Choral Performance

A Guide to Historical Practice

Steven E. Plank

The Scarecrow Press, Inc.
Lanham, Maryland • Toronto • Oxford
2004

SCARECROW PRESS, INC.

Published in the United States of America
by Scarecrow Press, Inc.
A wholly owned subsidiary of
The Rowman & Littlefield Publishing Group, Inc.
4501 Forbes Boulevard, Suite 200, Lanham, Maryland 20706
www.scarecrowpress.com

PO Box 317
Oxford
OX2 9RU, UK

British Library Cataloguing in Publication Information Available   .

Library of Congress Cataloging-in-Publication Data

Plank, Steven Eric.
   Choral performance : a guide to historical practice / Steven E. Plank.
      p. cm.
   Includes bibliographical references (p.   ) and index.
   ISBN 0-8108-5141-5 (pbk. : alk. paper)
   1. Choral singing—Interpretation (Phrasing, dynamics, etc.) 2.
Performance practice (Music) 3. Choral music—History. I. Title.
MT875.P53 2004
782.5'143—dc22

                                                                2004008272

∞™ The paper used in this publication meets the minimum requirements
of American National Standard for Information Sciences—Permanence of
Paper for Printed Library Materials, ANSI/NISO Z39.48-1992.
Manufactured in the United States of America.

for
Erika Plank Hagan
and
Aidan Andrews Plank

Whatever talents may be, if the man create not, the pure efflux of the Deity is not his—cinders and smoke there may be, but not yet flames.

—Ralph Waldo Emerson, *The American Scholar* (1837)

Contents

Acknowledgments

It is a pleasure to acknowledge the many debts of gratitude I have accumulated in the completion of this project. Some of the debts are long-standing ones to teachers, colleagues, family, and friends who have nurtured many of the ideas here in various ways. Some of the debts are more particular and immediate. I am grateful to Douglas Kirk (Montreal) and Daniel Davis (Rochester) for their kind assistance in obtaining source material. I am also grateful to my colleagues Richard Anderson (Oberlin), Alexander Blachly (Notre Dame), Jeffrey Gall (Oberlin), and Robert Longsworth (Oberlin) for helpful consultations. Particularly deep thanks go to my friend and colleague, Jack Ashworth (Louisville), who has read and commented on this study at length, lending along the way much insightful expertise and welcome advice. It is my very good fortune to have Bruce Phillips as an editor, and his guidance and encouragement of this project have been most noteworthy. It is also a great joy to acknowledge the contributions of the Collegium Musicum Oberliniense, with whom I have had the great privilege of performing early choral music since 1989. Their enthusiastic engagement of sixteenth-century polyphony has been a lasting inspiration, and much of the material in this book bears the stamp of our work together. My wife, Katherine Straney Plank, has, as in all things, been a sustaining presence; doubly so in this instance for her own extraordinary gifts in choral direction. I offer a final word of thanks to the Inn at Court Square in Charlottesville, Virginia, whose front porch provided an unusually pleasant autumnal venue in which to begin work on this study.

Musical examples from Clemens's Missa *Pastores quidnam vidistis* follow the edition of K. P. Bernet Kempers, *Clemens non Papa: Opera omnia* in *Corpus mensurabilis musicae* (1959), vol. 6, pp. 1–42, and are reproduced by kind permission of the American Institute of Musicology, Inc., of Middleton, Wisconsin.

Cover photograph:

Anon, Sixteenth-century Spanish. "The Fountain of Life." Detail.

Allen Memorial Art Museum, Oberlin College, Ohio. R. T. Miller Jr. Fund, 1952.

Chapter 1

Introduction

"Mind the gap" is a phrase made memorable for its frequent itera-tions on the London Underground. When a train pulls into its sta-tion, the hydraulic whoosh of opening doors and the clamor of the exiting throng have been traditionally accompanied by a calm, po-lite voice over the loudspeaker, requesting that one "mind the gap," that is, that one watch one's step and not trip on the space between train and platform. The phrase came to mind when I began the writ-ing of this book, because in a style-conscious culture, as ours surely is, there seem to be a number of gaps that await musical performers, and mindfully bridging those gaps—or at least navigating them—is an important, if not critical, part of modern interpretation. The par-ticular gap that motivates this study is the gap that often exists be-tween modern "mainstream" choral practitioners and historical modes of performance that offer a wide range of interpretative choice for premodern repertories. The visibility of historically in-formed performance is ubiquitous in our modern culture, and there are a number of signs of its increasing maturity. For example, the fact that the movement now habitually looks at itself historically and philosophically in thoughtful "meta-views" certainly represents a stage more advanced than the necessary first steps in which the gathering and interpretation of historical data was the unquestioned priority. With the maturation of the movement, the focus on ques-tions of "what" have been richly supplemented by questions of "how" and "why."[1] Moreover, the establishment of degree pro-grams,[2] the prominence of period ensembles, and the widening scope of the repertory to which historical modes of performance are fruitfully applied all suggest the robustness of the enterprise.

Regardless of its robustness and maturity, it is nevertheless an enterprise that is often on the other side of the "gap" from mainstream choral performance. And this is ironic, given the prominence of vocal ensemble music in premodern repertories and also the large part premodern music plays in the modern choral tradition. Prior to the seventeenth century, instrumental music, though often of high quality and ample quantity, frequently looked to vocal music for its models and its idioms. Moreover, the fact that much of this instrumental music was ephemeral and improvised has given it a second-class citizenship in a musical culture that tends to privilege written forms. On the other hand, the liturgical genres of mass and motet or the secular genres of madrigal and chanson represent Renaissance composition at its most mainstream. To an impressive degree, then, early music *is* vocal music, as the late Howard Mayer Brown long ago opined.[3] And if in looking back at music history we see an abundance of choral music, in looking from the other end of the telescope, we see that this repertory has had a strong claim on modern choirs. What oratorio chorus does not with regularity become Handelian? What school does not have some variation on the theme of "madrigal singers"? What church choir of nearly any stripe does not find the music of the gilded ages of Palestrina, Byrd, Schütz, Monteverdi, or Bach a formative part of their repertory?

It is thus surprising that the "gap" can be as wide as it often seems. Performance practice studies themselves seem to have dealt with instrumental repertories more readily than vocal ones, and specialist instrumental ensembles seem both to predate and outnumber specialist choirs. In part this reflects the fact that old instruments bring with them an aura of historicity. They come to us as (seemingly) objective artifacts from earlier times. Moreover, as the technology—the performing medium—is a formative factor in the performance practice, the instruments themselves have much to teach. Regrettably this is a source of instruction that vocal performance practice cannot hope to replicate; as Simon Ravens reminds, "In fairness to scholars of early vocal practices, we might point out that recognition of the violin's historical capabilities would not be quite so advanced had every early instrument been decaying for hundreds of years under six feet of soil."[4] The period instrument is assuredly not an infallible nor a complete instructor, but it is often a strikingly helpful guide that singers unfortunately cannot directly claim. In addition, the aura of objectivity that the instrumental artifact offers finds no corollary in the voice. The personal, subjective identity of the voice, period or otherwise, makes attempts to generalize from it difficult. And adding to the difficulty is that much as the violin has physically changed during its history, so too might we suspect the voice of the sixteenth century to be significantly different physiologically from its modern counterpart; what was easy and natural for one may not be so for the other.[5]

In a tangential way, the predominance of instrumental versus vocal emphasis in period performance may also have to do with marketing, at least in the first wave of historical recordings in the 1960s and 1970s. The crumhorn in hand is an unmistakable flag of association that could be promoted with ease. Upon seeing the crumhorn, the audience grows confident or at least expectant of a degree of historicity; on the other hand, the sight of a choir on stage tends to offer no similar clue. In addition, one could advertise a "first recording with original/authentic/period instruments"—an easy label to affix—whereas "first recording with original/authentic/period voices" crosses a line into nonsensical syntax. We cannot overestimate the role that marketability—in part, the ability to *label*—played in the nurture of the historical performance movement. Recording companies could trade on defamiliarization and novelty, and period instruments quickly stressed that what was to come was new and unfamiliar. The choir, regardless of its stylistic orientation, was a medium too familiar to be easily packaged in these terms.

Opinions will certainly vary concerning the importance of historical performance for choirs, and these opinions reflect widely ranging views on aesthetics and vocal flexibility, that is, on the capacity of a chorister to switch between styles and tone qualities in much the same manner as a violinist might move between modern and baroque violins, depending on the repertory. Tone quality is, of course, a component of "style," and one might embrace some components without crossing the gap into contentious questions of production and sound—these are interpretative choices—and, again, there seems no consensus apparent. In a 1980 survey of English choral conductors in the collegiate and cathedral traditions, Peter Phillips assembled a number of views. For example, Barry Rose of

St. Paul's Cathedral (London) advocated something akin to the "two violins" approach:

> The boys have two stops. We can sing Byrd's *Prevent us O Lord* and the Hallelujah Chorus in the same service and make the latter sound like the Royal Choral Society in full flight and the other like a very beautiful, ethereal choir. The boys simply make a different noise—different in timbre, different in production. For the big sound they tighten up in the throat slightly so that there is an increase in hardness and intensity, they take their chest-voices into the upper end of the range; and they know by my arms which sound I'm after.[6]

Sir David Willcocks, then only a few years removed from his tenure at King's College Cambridge, suggested stylistic flexibility, but one that did not extend to tone quality: "Of course you must adjust your style to suit that of the music . . . , but it is fussy and pernickety to expect a choir actually to alter the tone-quality it produces."[7] Similarly, Bernard Rose, *Informator choristarum* at Magdalen College, Oxford, hoped for a single sound that would work in all styles: "I believe that if you concentrate on pure and unanimous vowels, this will produce a sound which is appropriate and pleasant for every period of music."[8] Taking a different path, Edward Higginbottom of New College, Oxford, sought refuge not in historic aesthetics but rather in vocal health: "I do not attempt to get a certain sound because I believe it to be the right sound for a certain type of music, I seek a sound because I believe it to be the right way to sing."[9]

Thus four directors from a reasonably unified context with striking variability on the question at hand. The variability does not surprise us in a modern world, where individuality and freedom of choice are celebrated with vigor. In looking to the past, it is important to acknowledge—with equal vigor—that it too was heterogeneous. In dealing with the past, it is understandable to wish for tidy, idealized monoliths that we can manage, but that tidy view is, to borrow the phrasing of art critic Ada Louise Huxtable, "the replacement of reality with selective fantasy." The historical realities are full of variables; any other view is looking at some things and *not* looking at others. Huxtable's critical gaze is aimed at the manufactured historical tidiness of Colonial Williamsburg in Virginia, a theme park or a museum (depending on your attitude) of late eighteenth-century American life. She writes that Colonial Williamsburg "has perverted the way we think"; it has led Americans to prefer—and believe in—a sanitized and selective version of the past, to deny the diversity and eloquence of change and continuity, to ignore the actual deposits of history and humanity that make our cities vehicles of a special kind of art and experience, the gritty accumulations of the best and worst we have produced. This [historical] record has the wonder and distinction of being the real thing.[10]

And much as the *historical* Williamsburg does not look like the modern theme park, neither does historical performance practice look like unified, contextless "laws" awaiting allegiant adoption and enactment by modern interpreters. Historical performance that is based on history must begin by celebrating choice, not rules.[11] Works kept in the repertory decades after their composition—one thinks of Gregorio Allegri's "Miserere" or Cristobal Morales's "Lamentabatur Jacob" in the Capella Sistina or the centuries-long use of Gregorian chant, for instance—invite us to see reinterpretations that change with the context as *historical* realities, much as do the contrasting performance contexts that coexist within a single time frame. Add to this the contradictions in didactic sources, and even the most rule-inclined practitioner will be hard pressed to know where to place his unflagging allegiance.

Accordingly then, in inviting the modern choral musician to consider anew questions of historical performance practice, I will focus on range of choice, not constraint of idea. However, in balance, the heterogeneity of history is not chaotic, nor is it an interpretative free-for-all. Informed choice requires a knowledge of what the choices are and how those choices fit into aesthetic systems, historical and contemporary. The late Andrea von Ramm, long a powerfully expressive singer with the *Studio der frühen Musik*, compellingly reminds that it is often the lack of knowledge that constrains choice:

Historical music offers a vast choice of different periods, different languages, different social backgrounds, different musical instruments, different ideas of what beautiful singing means—differing from generation to generation, from country to country. Sometimes one forces all these differences into a single unit: our time, our personal interpretation. Every piece of music sounds the same, no matter who the composer is or what the intention of the composition is. In most cases singers don't have bad intentions when they sing everything the same. They simply do not know how to approach different styles in different ways.[12]

They simply do not know how to approach different styles in different ways. Knowledge, then, is the key, but one of the "gaps" of which we must be mindful is the gap that separates our historical knowledge, our performance intuition, and the practical realities of performance itself. Some years ago my colleagues and I were preparing a brochure to advertise our historical performance studies program to prospective Conservatory students, and each of us was solicited to come up with some memorable quotations—the hoped-for spice amid the necessarily bland prose of curricular requirements, course offerings, and the like. After reflecting a while, I decided I wanted to acknowledge the "gap" but also the interaction of the elements it separates. Thus, I offered: "Historical performance is a dance where creative leaps of faith, individual expression, and historical documentation learn to be partners with one another. The choreography is wonderfully flexible, the dance itself stimulating, and the results exhilarating." The language seems to me now a bit exuberant—it tries too hard to be quotable—but I nevertheless continue to be much taken with the notion that there *is* a choreography of elements, and that notions of historical performance rooted primarily in documentation sadly reduce a rich ensemble "dance" to a constrained effort by one alone. This "solo effort" may be virtuosic—that is, the documentary flair may be impressive—but alone it is sadly lacking what the other elements bring.

Yet for it all, I suspect that things objective and documentable—a form of musical literalism—are at the apex of our historical hierarchies. As recently as 1995, Peter Kivy observed that, "Historical reasons have begun to overpower what might be called 'reasons of the ear' to the extent that it no longer seems intellectually respectable, in musical circles, to adduce reasons of the ear *against* the claims of historical authenticity."[13] From the standpoint of musical performance—especially of the Renaissance—this is somewhat ironic in that one of the striking distinctions of fifteenth-century aesthetics is precisely the liberation of the ear to make aesthetic judgments. Edward Lowinsky, in a compelling essay from 1966, underscored this point as a major distinction between the Middle Ages and the Renaissance:

> It is, of course, a truism that music, at all times, and also during the Middle Ages, was an art of the ear. . . . [But] what happens when demands of the ear conflict with those of mathematics? . . . [In the Re-

naissance] personal experience now becomes a valid point of departure. . . . [I]t is in the Renaissance that the conflict between the ear and mathematics in matters musical is not only openly acknowledged but often no less openly resolved in favor of the ear.[14]

A representative contemporary view would be that of Johannes Tinctoris, who in his *Terminorum musicae diffinitorium* (Treviso, 1495), defined harmony as "any amenity in sound," amenity (*amoenitas*) being a subjective quality.[15] In other words, if we are to be guided in our approach to Renaissance music by contemporaneous sensibilities, then we must fully acknowledge the role of the ear and other subjective aspects in formulating a performance practice.[16] And we might ask, if history is to claim our allegiance, is documentation the exclusive way there?[17]

Several modern commentators underscore that one way we learn about historical performance is *in the doing*. For example, the venerable Josef Mertin, a Viennese pioneer in the field, prefaces his monograph, *Early Music: Approaches to Performance Practice*, with the statement, "[W]e arrive at decisive insights only by active musical realization of a work." And he echoes this in the preludial confession that "[A]lthough I personally learned a great deal from [the scholars] Adler, Ficker, and Fischer, I am writing as a conductor and not as a musicologist."[18] Similarly, John Potter strikes an experiential note with advice concerning ensemble singing: "Discussing the music is often helpful, but it isn't the only way to decide how things go. Everyone will absorb and communicate various ideas about the piece simply by singing it."[19] Accordingly, a choreography between sources, experiential and written, seems fruitful in formulating a performance practice. However, it is important to note that the pitfalls of projecting modern experience onto historical circumstance are many, for historical and modern subjective experiences remain two very different things, and the latter will not necessarily unlock the daunting mysteries of the former.

In reflecting on both the ideas of "choreography" and "gaps," I have been especially taken with the image on the title page of Franchinus Gaffurius's treatise, *Practica musicae utiusque cantus . . .* (1512). The representation shows a monastic choir gathered around a common lectern, from which they sing the chant versicle, "Benedicamus." Much in the image contrasts with our modern music-making, most notably the common page and the absence of a conductor (although hands on the shoulders of youths suggest time-keeping by more senior members of the choir). But something in the image seems ironically to illumine the modern situation. In the lower right-hand corner, apart from the choir, sits a youth engrossed in a book and with two formidable volumes by his side. In context of the image itself, he is perhaps a student, maybe even one learning to read as a preliminary to admission into the choir. But with historical hindsight, he also seems to emblematize a familiar performance practice situation. Someone with a book—the written evidence—is placed in the context of performance, the experience of music-making, though he clearly remains apart from it, critiquing and informing perhaps, but distinct and separate from the experience and action. The someone with the book potentially has much to offer, but the *gap* between himself and the singers is a critical one to bridge.[20]

Written and documentable evidence forms the bedrock of our understanding of historical style. When we perform historical repertories, however, the very act of performance itself moves us beyond a dutiful literalism, and in this we share a spirit with Renaissance performers who, though sometimes guided by the written treatise, were not driven to it by a "historical" sense.[21]

This is nicely illustrated in Kivy's distinctions between "sonic authenticity" on the one hand and "sensible authenticity" on the other. A sonic authenticity would replicate the sound of a period performance, and presumably in an objectively verifiable manner. However, the way in which a modern audience receives this sound—the effect it has on them, the impression it makes—may be quite distant from that of the period audience, even though the objective sounds are the same. In this case, then, sensible authenticity has escaped. Kivy's example is of two audiences hearing sonically identical performances of Bach's St. Matthew Passion. In the literal sense, there is but one performance. However, the period audience may be struck *sensibly* by the scale and loudness of, say, the opening chorus; the modern audience, on the other hand hears in those very same sounds the intimacy of chamber music. The sonically authentic (literalistic) performance may then recapture historical means, but in doing so, it may ironically obliterate historical ends.[22] If the historical intention is, say, grandeur, period forces, which must vie against subsequent modern connotations of grandeur, may find it difficult to achieve the historical effect. Which is the higher calling, the sonic authenticity or the sensible authenticity? It is difficult to imagine a more difficult question for practitioners of historical performance. And the difficulty lies in the different answers that can assert a historical claim. For some repertories, it is easy to imagine the priority of the sonically authentic. Early English polyphony of the fifteenth century, for instance, seems to glory in sound for sound's sake, reveling in new manners of aural sweetness. Indeed, a Marian motet by John Dunstable may claim a liturgical/spiritual function, but given the novelty of the very distinctive sound, it is difficult not to see the sound itself as an unusually high priority. On the other hand, a Palestrina motet may be richly sonic but perhaps ultimately more essentially a spiritual gesture than an exercise in sound. And it is close historical study that can help one navigate the distance between them. The gap between sonic and sensible authenticity is striking and challenging . . . another formidable gap of which to be mindful.[23] Clearly both have a strong claim in formulating an interpretation, although the priorities each asserts will vary with context and interpretative goal.

What follows in chapters 2 through 8 is a look at a number of issues in which premodern choral technique and performance practice are distinctively different from their modern counterparts—timbre, tempo and rhythm, makeup of the ensemble, articulation, ornamentation, pitch, and tuning. The look is decidedly selective; the focus is largely on Renaissance repertory and sources, both for the richness with which they exemplify and treat the issues at hand, and also in acknowledgment that it is in the Renaissance that choral performance gains its first blossoming.[24] Neither is the intent proscriptive. Rather, the discussion aims to promote interpretative choice, hoping that by clarifying and broadening the range of choices, modern interpreters will engage this repertory with added insight and creative richness. The approach draws on scholarship and historical source material, as certainly the subject matter requires, but it also draws on my own personal experience of performing and teaching this repertory, as certainly the subject matter also requires.

Finally, a word about audience. It is my hope that this study will be of interest to musicians who specialize in early music, but primarily it is addressed to conductors and singers who come to "early music" from the mainstream and perform it in that context. Faced with the need to develop multiple styles of performance to meet the expressive needs of their broad repertory, mainstream choral conductors will find historical style an essential element to consider, and hopefully a congenial ally in the act of interpretation.

NOTES

1. For a history of the movement, see Harry Haskell's engaging *The Early Music Revival: A History* (London: Thames & Hudson, 1988); for philosophical investigations of the nature of historical performance, see, inter alia, Laurence Dreyfus, "Early Music Defended against Its Devotees," *Musical Quarterly* 69 (1983): 297–322; Peter Kivy, *Authenticities: Philosophical Reflections on Musical Performance* (Ithaca, N.Y.: Cornell University Press, 1995); Nicholas Kenyon, ed., *Authenticity and Early Music: A Symposium* (London: Oxford University Press, 1988); Richard Taruskin, *Text and Act: Essays on Music and Performance* (New York: Oxford University Press, 1995); John Butt, *Playing with History* (Cambridge: Cambridge University Press, 2002); and the often probing interviews collected in Bernard Sherman's *Inside Early Music: Conversations with Performers* (New York: Oxford University Press, 1997).

2. Degree programs in the United States include those at Oberlin College, Case Western Reserve University, Boston University, the University of Southern California, and Indiana University.

3. "[W]e ought always to be aware of the fact that early music means vocal music in the first place." "Choral Music in the Renaissance," *Early Music* 6 (1978): 164.

4. "A Sweet Shrill Voice: The Countertenor and Vocal Scoring in Tudor England," *Early Music* 26 (1998): 123. Cf. also John Potter's observation of how instrumental forces can seem advanced of vocal ones in terms of historical grounding: "Some aspects of early music singing have seemed anachronistic, such as the muddled attempts to re-create Baroque gesture or the strange coupling of highly researched instrumental playing with academically under-nourished singers." *The Cambridge Companion to Singing* (Cambridge: Cambridge University Press, 2000), 3.

5. Cf. Ravens, "A Sweet Shrill Voice," 124, which weds questions of vocal pitch, laryngeal size, and physical height in a context of changing historical norms.

6. Peter Phillips, "The Golden Age Regained 2," *Early Music* 8 (1980): 183.

7. Phillips, "Golden Age 2," 183.

8. Phillips, "Golden Age 2," 183

9. Phillips, "Golden Age 2," 183.

10. In Richard Handler and Eric Gable, *The New History in an Old Museum: Creating the Past at Colonial Williamsburg* (Durham, N.C.: Duke University Press, 1997), 44.

11. The point elicits frequent comment. See, for example Eleanor Self-ridge-Field: "Our historical perception of the period 1600 to 1750 as a unified whole has encouraged us to search for all-embracing answers where (for the most part) none exists, and where greater aesthetic value is attached to variety than to consistency." In Jeffrey Kurtzman, *The Monteverdi Vespers of 1610: Music, Context, and Performance* (Oxford: Oxford University Press, 1999), 347.

12. "Singing Early Music," *Early Music* 4 (1976): 12.

13. Kivy, *Authenticities,* x.

14. "Music of the Renaissance as Viewed by Renaissance Musicians," in *The Renaissance Image of Man and the World*, ed. Bernard O'Kelly (Columbus: Ohio State University Press, 1966), 136.

15. See *Dictionary of Musical Terms,* trans. Carl Parrish (New York: Free Press of Glencoe, 1963), 8–9. See also Rob Wegman, "Sense and Sensibility in Late-Medieval Music," *Early Music* 23 (1995): 299–312.

16. Cf. Morris Berman's provocative advocacy of somatic history in *Coming to Our Senses: Body and Spirit in the Hidden History of the West* (New York: Bantam, 1989), esp. chapter 3, "The Body of History."

17. Cf. Kivy, *Authenticities,* 41. "'[H]ard evidence' is not the sum total of historical research in general or of music-historical research in particular. And there are those with a talent for the imaginative leap from the physical artifact to the mind that made it. That too is history, not fiction—the kind of history that can give us the insight we need to answer such questions as it is necessary to raise if we are to have a full-blooded notion of what the composer really wished or intended with regard to performance."

Regarding our privileging of written information, see, inter alia, the interesting discussion in Neil Postman's *Amusing Ourselves to Death* (New York: Penguin, 1985), 20–21. Postman tellingly recounts the story of a graduate student's thesis defense at which his examining committee took exception to a footnote that carefully documented a spoken conversation. The committee's accusation of "journalism," not scholarship, was countered by the student's question that if they had accepted the veracity of the hundreds of footnotes documenting written sources, why would they suspect anything less in the one conversational source. Their reply spoke volumes about the prevailing contemporary attitude, as they responded with another question: Assuming that he passed his exam, would he like the committee to write that fact down somewhere, or rather just tell someone?

18. Trans. Siegmund Levarie (Irig, 1978; reprint, New York: Da Capo Press, 1986), xiii.

19. Potter, *Companion*, 163. The experiential path toward historical performance practice will on occasion be graced with the fruits of "accidental historicism," that is, the serendipitous discovery of a historical mode brought about for reasons other than the historical. One resident of Colonial

Williamsburg wrote of precisely this point in 1931: "Those of us who have lately removed an old picket fence, or obliterated the traces of an old smoke house which was falling down in the backyard, are overcome by shame and remorse, while others who have not been able to afford new front steps or to have a little attic room remade, with a higher ceiling, are filled with pride as if their actions had been restrained by good taste and correct knowledge instead of a lean purse." Handler and Gable, *New History*, 35.

20. For a reproduction of the image, see the frontispiece to Timothy J. McGee, *Medieval and Renaissance Music: A Performer's Guide* (Toronto: University of Toronto Press, 1985).

21. Cf. Potter, *Companion*, 3: "There are also signs that singers are having the courage to break away from slavish adherence to musicological dogma and are beginning to think more like their medieval and Renaissance predecessors (who the evidence suggests, generally preferred the delights of emotional self-indulgence to the musicology of their own day"). Cf. also Pierre Boulez: "By all means let there be a library, but a library which exists only as required. It must be a 'library in flames,' one which is perpetually reborn from its ashes in an always elusive, unforeseeable form. Must the flame at the heart of this library be tamed, preserved and sanctified within a temple protected by restrictions? Or, on the other hand, must one for ever be forced to steal it, spreading the fire at the risk of being consumed by it?" "The Vestal Virgin and the Fire-stealer: Memory, Creation and Authenticity," *Early Music* 18 (1990): 358.

22. See Kivy, *Authenticities*, 189, 231. An interesting literary example of this idea surfaces in Jose Luis Borges's story, "Pierre Menard, Author of the Quixote," in *Labyrinths* (New York: New Directions, 1986), 36–44. In the story, the twentieth-century writer, Menard, assumes the "mysterious duty of reconstructing" Cervantes's "spontaneous work" of *Don Quixote*. (p. 41), that is, of writing the same text as Cervantes anew. Tellingly, as the story illustrates, equality of surface content—the same words—does not lead to equality of meaning and style; written by a seventeenth-century Spaniard they mean one thing, by a twentieth-century Frenchman, another. I am grateful to my colleague, Jack Ashworth, for referring me to the story.

23. One easily perceived manifestation of sonic–sensible distinctions surfaces in the way that historical performance often trades on its ability to render the familiar unfamiliar, and in so doing, restore to a work a measure of its original sensible freshness, regardless of the degree to which it is sonically authentic.

24. See the classic Manfred Bukofzer, "The Beginnings of Choral Polyphony," in *Studies in Medieval and Renaissance Music* (New York: W. W. Norton, 1950).

Chapter 2

"It's on Account of the Sound It Is"

In a wonderful reflection on "musemathematics," James Joyce's memorable character Bloom reflects:

> Musemathematics. And you think you're listening to the ethereal. But suppose you said it like: Martha, seven times nine minus x is thirty-five thousand. Falls quite flat. It's on account of the sound it is.[1]

Much as Bloom relocates the lyrical magic in sound rather than arithmetical metaphysics, it is the *sound* of early music singing that is perhaps its most distinctive element. Questions of timbre and tone quality most quickly separate modern and premodern technique and also comprise one of the most alluring aspects of early music. Long before one comes to appreciate historical claims, etc., the sound of the music itself attracts, satisfies, and beguiles. That this is so is perhaps much the fruit of its being different from the mainstream—the attraction of the unfamiliar and the novel—but the aesthetic of tone quality so often associated with premodern music has, in its purity and sweetness, a rich claim on the modern ear. However, it is also critical to underscore that if one can generalize an aesthetic of purity and sweetness—an "early music choral sound," so to speak—it is a generalization that will not fit all contexts or historical paradigms. Amending Bloom then, more properly in our case, "it's on account of the sound*s*, it is." Timbre and tone quality may be distinctive, but they are scarcely monolithic, and as we have outlined in chapter 1, it is the range of choice rather than dogmatic proscription that will concern us here.

The discussion of tone quality is challenging for many reasons; the subjective nature of sound, the challenge of translating nonverbal entities into words, and the absence of a historical voice as a sound source, a sonic artifact surviving from history, all defy an ease of approach. Although the passing of time may well alter the sound of a historical instrument, and although different players may get stunningly different sounds from one and the same instrument, nevertheless, the objective nature of a historical instrument as opposed to the voice invites us to interpret it as a somewhat reliable guide to the sounds of the past. Historical voices, even if they were not now "six feet under," cannot claim that same degree of objectivity. Accordingly, it is tempting to attempt to formulate vocal sounds based on what we know of instrumental colors and qualities. The basic point of departure has tended to be that instrumentalists aspire to imitate the voice, and to the degree that this is so, their imitation may lead us back to the original thing. Moreover, the frequency of collaboration between instruments and voices, as well as the interpenetrability of idioms, also suggests they shared a common sound aesthetic.

The sound of early instruments is often characterized by a high degree of focus to the sound, a leanness of tone quality that is often accompanied by a high degree of shapely vowel in the sound. Although we have come to think of early instruments as quieter than their modern counterparts—in many cases an unproblematic assumption—the range of volume with early instruments is significant. Outdoor instruments, like the shawm, for instance, readily confirm that a full range of volume was available, though its availability was much guided by context.[2]

Certain modern commentators have attempted to associate instrumental sounds with vocal qualities. For example, the Italian organist Luigi Tagliavini describes the *ripieno* of early Italian organs as "a silvery and light sound that is never aggressive . . . [with a] voicing that is lively and sweet at the same time," and in so doing notes that it is an "instrumental interpretation of a choral ensemble."[3] Renaissance commentators were led in similar directions. Writers such as Conrad von Zabern and Heinrich Finck suggest that as the organ has many pipes of various sizes, the voice corresponds with a diversity of sound according to register: In the low range there should be a fullness of sound, in the middle range, a moderate sound, and in the high range, the sound should be soft. Thus, uniformity of sound throughout the range is eschewed, in favor of variety of dynamic and presumably of color. Finck writes that, "one should know that whosoever would sing beautifully and with understanding has to use his voice in three shades [full, moderate, and soft, by register]," and he likens this to the variety of organ pipes:

> Now man does not have as many pipes in him, but just one throat through which the voice is produced; and this one organ must produce all those different shades of tone! What a lack of judgement it is to wish to bring this about through a continued uniform use of one and the same organ![4]

Timbral variety, such as Finck describes, is one component of what we might call an "aesthetic of diversity" that has a number of musical manifestations in Renaissance music. Variety of articulation and frequent recourse to ornamentation also come immediately to mind.[5]

Instrumental analogies, once again, offer a measure of concreteness that is attractive. Verbal descriptions are more elusive and often harder to translate into sound. Nonetheless, since the Middle Ages, writers have responded to the challenge. In the twelfth century, Bernard of Clairvaux, for instance, in a sermon on the *Song of Songs*—rapturous biblical love poetry—urges a liturgical singing style that is both strong and lacking in nasality. To the choir singers he urged that they should proceed

> not as lazy, sleepy or bored creatures, not sparing your voices, not cutting off half the words or omitting some altogether, nor with voices broken or weak, neither singing through the nose with an effeminate lisp, but bringing forth with virile resonance and affection voices worthy of the Holy Spirit.[6]

Bernard's admonition for "virile resonance" may be born of the highly gendered dialogue of the *Song of Songs,* with the singers here adopting a particularly masculine tone in the service of the church as the allegorically feminine bride. (The *Song of Songs* texts have historically received a variety of allegorical interpretations that see the female beloved as variously the Christian Soul, the Church, or the Blessed Virgin Mary, among others.)[7] But it also is consistent with oft-repeated, later counsel that singing in church was full, presumably to address the large spaces of ecclesiastical buildings.[8] The critical reference to nasality is noteworthy, especially as attempts at a highly focused sound, following the lead of instruments, can take one, though not of necessity, in that direction. One particularly striking reference to nasality in medieval singing appears in Chaucer's *The Canterbury Tales*. In the "General Prologue" to the tales, the Prioresse is described as singing the Office very well with seemly nasality:

> Ful weel she soong the service dyvyne,
> Entuned in hir nose ful semely[9]

That she is described singing the Office "ful weel" and that her nasal tone is described as "ful semely" seems, on the surface, to endorse this type of resonance. However, following David Wulstan's lead,[10] we might be led to the opposite conclusion, for Chaucer's portrayal of the prioress seems ironic and satirical. Her many qualities emerge as exaggerations: table manners that are unusually fastidious (At mete wel ytaught was she with alle:/She leet no morsel from hir lippes falle,/Ne wette hir fyngres in hir sauce depe;/Wel koude she carie a morsel and wel kepe/That no drope ne fille upon hire brest./In curteisie was set ful muchel hir lest./Hir over-lippe wyped she so clene/That in hir coppe ther was no ferthyng sene") and compassion that is extreme ("She was so charitable and so pitous/She wolde wepe, if that she saugh a mous/Kaught in a trappe, if it were deed or bledde."). Moreover, her standing is demeaned with the reference to her French: She spoke after the manner of "Stratford atte Bowe," for "Frenssh of Parys was to hire unknowe." If then Chaucer mocks her, her nasal singing may well be mockable in terms of contemporary taste, as well.[11]

Some medieval descriptions suggest that tone, as well as interpretation, might follow the affective sense of what is being sung. For example, the ninth-century *musica enchiriadis* suggests that

> In peaceful subjects let the notes be peaceful, happy in joyous matters, grieving in sad ones; let cruel words or deeds be expressed with harsh sounds—sudden, loud and swift—shaped according to the nature of events and the emotions.[12]

Here, as above, we note evidence of an aesthetic of variety; moreover, the mention of "harsh sounds" suggests perhaps a greater range of expression than is typically imagined. The affective guide to tone quality was certainly not limited to the Middle Ages. In a chant treatise from the early sixteenth century, for instance, Biagio Rossetti notes that liturgical tracts dealing with "toil and affliction" ought to be sung "slowly with harshness of voice [*cum asperitate vocum*]."[13]

The asperity of voice seems to be a special effect, elicited by subject. Isidore esteems the voice that is "high, sweet and loud: high to be adequate to the sublime; loud to fill the ear; sweet to soothe the minds of the hearers."[14] And it is sweetness that seems to occupy the attention of many commentators in subsequent generations. In hymning the qualities of the musical Renaissance, Tinctoris savors sweetness repeatedly.[15] For him sweetness is the quality of the new consonant counterpoint emerging in the fifteenth century, but also it attaches, one presumes, to the quality with which that counterpoint is sung. Later, in the seventeenth century, the quality of sweetness is once again being affirmed. Marin Mersenne, in his important encyclopedia, *Harmonie Universelle* (1636), continues this line of thinking:

> There are several other qualities that one can desire in the voice, and which one finds rather seldom, for example, the sweetness and certain harmony upon which depend the charms which ravish the listeners, because voices which are hard do not please, even though they be accurate . . . because they are too piercing and fierce.[16]

Here the sweetness is a critical element in affective response—the foundation of seventeenth-century music. If the writers affirm sweetness, as they seem to do without equivocation, knowing what sweetness of tone specifically refers to is, however, not altogether clear. Is it simply an amenity in sound? (And thus, do notions of sweetness change with the context?) Note for instance the complexity of the issue that arises when Charles Butler, in 1636, describes the countertenor voice: "The Countertenor or Contratenor, is so called, because it answereth the Tenor, though commonly in higher keys: and therefore is fittest for a man of a sweet shrill voice."[17] In our common expectations, the qualities of shrillness and sweetness pull against each other, for the former comes often with the sense of a piercing pungency. And while the combination may simply suggest a sweet highness of range, that it *may* not confirms the difficulty of basing tone quality on verbal description.

Issues of timbre are closely related to issues of blend. For some repertories, this seems to be a critical quality. For example, in imitative counterpoint of the sixteenth century, one aesthetic point of departure is the equality of voices. The web of counterpoint intertwines a consort of equals, and though this is most objectively clear in the melodic equality of parts—everybody has the same melodic motives—it is difficult not to extend that both to dynamics and timbre, given the degree of equality that so clearly exists melodically.

It is perhaps the case that we have located blend too exclusively in the realm of dynamics,[18] whereas tone quality itself is as vital an element in achieving a well-balanced ensemble. Conversely, where certain compositional styles privilege certain lines, to bring them out only through louder dynamics suggests too limited an approach. Distinction of timbres as a device to single out individual lines is a valuable tool in conveying the architectural hierarchies in less "democratically" inclined pieces. Wulstan has drawn attention to various pieces in which the text underlay strategically juxtaposes different vowels, and thus different timbres, to creative effect.[19]

The awareness of vowels as a color element underscores the important and increasingly prominent sensitivity to period pronunciation in historical performance. As with the use of period instruments, period pronunciation brings with it the overtones of historicity, and as with period performance in general, it has the dynamic capacity to defamiliarize the familiar; to introduce, at least at this point, novel sounds, regardless of historic claims. But certainly much of the attraction of period pronunciation is the vastly expanded range of color that emerges through the text.[20] Distinctions of chronology—"old" French vis-à-vis modern French, for example —introduce many significant changes, but also national versions of a notably unstandardized Latin vary the palette considerably. Moreover, regional accents of the same language also show important differences. In the end, the rich variety of vowel and diphthong offer a range of sounds and color that can make the uniform purity of standardized Roman Latin seem pale by comparison.

Closely related to the question of color and critical to concepts of sound is the question of vibrato, long one of the "hot spots" in the discussion of early vocal style, even to the point where, one suspects, its relative absence or presence has become a litmus test for stylistic orthodoxy. Recently articulated views strike a moderate tone. Ellen Hargis, for instance, acknowledges that it is "the thorniest issue to confront the singer of early music," and notes that "it is now generally accepted that a gentle vibration of the voice is natural and expressive. . . . It is really the degree of [breath] pressure and pitch obfuscation that is the problem with modern vibrato.[21] And while opinions in both historical sources and modern commentary will vary, all will agree that the use and the degree of use of vibrato can radically affect our sense of a work.[22]

Comment on vibrato is chronologically wide-ranging. Jerome of Moravia, in his thirteenth-century *Tractatus de musica,* describes an ornamental vibrato, "a harmonic flower, . . . a very swift and storm-like vibration."[23] And the notion that vibrato is something that might be applied with discretion as occasion and context demand, as opposed to an ongoing, continuous feature of the sound, is one of the chief contrasts between historical and modern notions of vibrato. An interesting analogy might be made with the use of organ tremulants. Italian sources, like Diruta and Antegnati, suggest their employment in special circumstances—music that is slow, unornamented, or mournful.[24] In other words, they were not pervasively used. Moreover, that Antegnati mentions the tremulant in context of unornamented passage work may also suggest that the tremulant itself becomes the ornamental factor contributing its own kind of adornment. Adding weight to the analogy is the compelling point that where Italian organs seem most self-consciously "vocal" is in the registration of the *vox humana*, which combines two registers with one tuned sharp in order to create a shimmering, gentle beating effect. Thus when the organ tried to represent the human voice, it did so with vibrato, but vibrato was reserved for a special effect. Showing again the notion that vibrato might be discretionary is Lodovico Zacconi's advice in his 1592 *Prattica di musica.* He writes that "the tremolo, that is the trembling voice, is the true gate to enter the passages and to become proficient in the *gorgia* . . . the tremolo should be short and beautiful, for if it is long and forceful, it tires and bores."[25] Obviously Zacconi is recommending a sparing use, for overuse causes the vibrato to lose its interest. Integral to the use of vibrato as ornament, or expressive device, is the notion that vibrato in the sound *is* controllable, and thus, can be tapped at will.[26] Andrea von Ramm, the pioneering and ultra-expressive soprano with *Studio der frühen Musik,* brought a no-nonsense tone to the issue: "The so-called natural vibrato does not exist. Vibrato is an interaction of breathing muscles and throat muscles and can be controlled."[27]

It is this notion of control that emerges in the writings of the French music encyclopedist, Marin Mersenne, who extols evenness, as well as accuracy and flexibility. In the *Harmonie Universelle* he comments on what might make a teacher think a student would be a good one to teach:

> As to their qualities, they should be accurate, even and flexible; accuracy consists in starting the pitch neither higher nor lower than the note desired. Evenness is holding the voice firm and stable on the same tone *without wavering*, but one may sing the tone louder or softer as long as one stays on pitch; and flexibility of the voice is nothing other than the facility and disposition for making all the degrees or intervals of the scale, ascending or descending, and in making all kinds of passages and diminutions.[28]

The great German music encyclopedist Michael Praetorius cites a "pleasantly vibrating voice" as a requisite for the singer, but notes as well the necessity that this quality be moderate—"not . . . as some are trained to do in schools, but with particular moderation."[29] Although at first reading, Praetorius's meaning seems clear, there are varying interpretations. Some suggest that he has perhaps an intensity vibrato, rather than a pitch fluctuation, in mind.[30] Praetorius's requisites were repeated by Johann Andreas Herbst in his 1642 *Musica Practica sive instructio,* and later underscored in treatises from the last part of the century by Wolfgang Mylius and Georg Falck.[31]

What emerges in the sources, then, is a range of views on vibrato, encompassing unwavering steadiness, ornamental gesture, moderate presence, and unqualified tremulousness. Given the range, what might guide the performer's choice? Contexts will certainly offer different possibilities. Solo singing, with its capacity and freedom for ornamentation, might well employ vibrato judiciously as an ornamental grace, whereas choral singing, much less often ornamental for reasons of ensemble, might less often find it fruitful. The musical style may also be highly influential. Renaissance counterpoint, with its aesthetic of geometric clarity, for instance, seems to emerge with greater clarity in straighter tones. Acknowledging the range of opinion, one must still affirm that, Praetorius aside, the usage seems to have been historically conservative and seems not to have approached the continuous vibrato of modern technique.

Perhaps the greatest reason in support of straight-tone singing, however, relates to pitch and tuning. The modern tuning system can more readily absorb pan-vibrato, for in a fully tempered system, all notes are a bit out of tune in order to secure maximum harmonic flexibility. Their slight out-of-tuneness introduces beats in the sound that blur the clarity of the tuning and are sympathetic to the wavering beats of vibrato. However, the prevailing tuning systems of the Renaissance and Baroque are based on pure, beatless intervals, which grace the harmony with pristine clarity. To introduce a singing style that *adds* beats injudiciously is to veil and obfuscate the very thing upon which the tuning is based. One may extend the concern to the pitch integrity of the individual notes as well; that is, it is not only the vertical combination of pitches that suffers but also the horizontal pitches themselves. Gaffurius, for instance, avers that "tones having a wide and ringing vibrato" are problematic because "these tones do not maintain a true pitch."[32]

The above view seems to give priority to intonation and tuning over linear elements that vibrato might enhance. It is a good example of the need to establish hierarchies of values, and they are hierarchies that are mutable from style to style, context to context. Bruno Turner, the founding conductor of the Pro Cantione Antiqua of London, raised precisely this issue of rival elements in singing. He noted:

> The new religion is no vibrato, and that is rubbish. Less vibrato is a good thing, but whoever authorized no vibrato? Counterpoint is only one element in the music; there is expression too and you should allow your voice to be coloured and not sing like an automaton. That is the danger with no vibrato . . . we want the voice to be vibrant and full of rich tones, not thick; there is a difference between wobble and being rich.
>
> Clarity is fine; but I feel some non-vibrato performances exhibit a new vice of being over-straight and lack the natural shaping and breathing inherent in the music. Passion and warmth are not inappropriate in church polyphony.[33]

One wonders if the specter of the automaton, the vice of being overstraight, weighs disproportionately heavy on the minds of skeptical modern singers, and that their fear is in reality the sound of a straw man's voice. Straight-tone singing that is well supported and the product of a relaxed vocal mechanism need not sound forced, flat, or characterless; when combined with careful note shaping, a strong sense of linear contour, dynamic gesture, and the interplay of strikingly demarcated vowels, the resulting sound can be fully alive, animated, and expressive.[34]

Various types of vibrato, of course, offer different attractions and present different problems. In earlier repertories, as we discussed above, pitch-vibrato, that is, the trilling fluctuation of pitches, is problematic in a style that benefits from clarity of counterpoint and purity of intonation. An intensity vibrato, however, produced by the diaphragm, can enrich the sound, and used with discretion is a creative part of the expressive vocabulary.

One of the vectors one may follow in a diachronic look at music history is the demonstrable increase in the volume of sound and the continuing mechanical adaptation to meet those needs. The history of the piano, for instance, sees a move to an instrument with a metal frame, heavier hammers and strings, and increased string tension, equipping itself to fill large halls and compete with the volume level of symphony orchestras, whose instruments themselves have also been adapted to greater carrying power with larger bores in the winds and heightened bridges, increased string tension, and stronger bass bars in the strings. While these are mechanical responses to a change in both aesthetic and the social context (a move from intimate chambers to large concert halls), the voice must also respond to those same changes in context and aesthetic without, obviously, the possibility of change in the construction of the mechanism. But the way in which the physiological mechanism is used is clearly adaptive. Singing at "modern" levels of volume benefits from high, constant breath pressure. The constant vibrato that characterizes modern technique is a corollary to this; it is necessary in order to provide fluctuations that help the vocal mechanism withstand the sustained high breath pressure. Presumably, earlier repertories and venues do not require the expanded volume of sound that we associate with modern singing, and accordingly, one presumes, a lower, more relaxed breath pressure obtains. With that more relaxed, lower breath pressure, the physiological *need* for continuous vibrato is obviated. Significantly, attempts at straight-tone singing *with* high breath pressure can produce a problematic tension, but again, the high breath pressure required on the modern opera stage is rarely, if ever, required in the more intimate contexts of earlier repertories. Moreover, certain schools in premodern technique favor a low breath pressure that is variable, rather than constant. This contrast to modern technique, with its constant spinning of a steady stream of air, also leads to a relaxation of both mechanism and sound.[35]

Historical comment is occasionally quite specific with regard to breath pressure. For example, Padre Cerone, in his treatise *El Melopeo y maestro* (1613), notes that "[w]hen one begins to study singing, one should not drive the voice with the full force of the breath, and above all not too high. Rather one should produce tone according to his ability with moderate support. For strong forced singing damages the vocal apparatus and injures the windpipe."[36] Cerone's comment addresses beginning singers, but the admonitions against a yelling type of singing are frequent, and from them we may glean the broad support for singing with lower breath pressure.[37]

The minimalist approach to vibrato encourages clarity not only of pitch and harmony but also of timbre, itself. The leanness of sound, the incisive edge, the focus and forwardness of the sound remain unveiled by the blur of vibrato. This clarity of sound is also encouraged by an elevated placement of the larynx, and this is a strong contrast to certain modern approaches. Several schools of modern singing advocate a lowered or depressed larynx to achieve fullness, richness, and roundness of tone. Singing with a depressed larynx is, however, relatively modern, arising only in the first part of the nineteenth century with the advocacy of Manuel Garcia.[38] Achieved in part by the tucking in of the chin,[39] it has the effect of homogenizing or blending the vowels into an artificial sameness and hampers agility; modern singers who favor it seem willingly to pay this price for the enriched resonance and depth of sound that results. Moreover, as a complement to the characteristically high breath pressure of modern singing, the depressed larynx stiffens the vocal folds so that they more easily withstand the breath pressure.[40] An elevated laryngeal position, on the other hand, well mated with lower breath pressure, produces a leanness of sound in which agility (musical and textual) is enhanced and vowel distinction strikingly and compellingly enriched. The result is not only clearer articulation of the text but also an expressive timbral variety that occurs with radically differentiated vowels.

NURTURING THE SOUND

In developing a historically informed sound, one of the gaps to be bridged is moving from the verbal description in the sources to real sound. The exercises and rehearsal techniques below are fruitful in building a fundamental sound that is useful as a sound base for various early repertories. Once again, it is not a question of building "*the* early music sound"—there is no such singularity—but rather of establishing fundamentals that position singers to adapt well to the timbral requirements of various early sounds.

(1) Tonal Focus

The leanness and high degree of focus that is often ideal are frequently the result of forward placement of the sound, and exercises that maximize the use of an initial "n" are beneficial in bringing the sound forward (Example 2.1).

Exercise 1

Example 2.1. Focus exercise

Use the drone to "find" the place where the sound feels as though it is hanging on the front of the facial mask. Hold it initially until all are placing it far enough forward. Those singing the pentachord should feel as though their initial *nee* grows out of that established by the drone. Listen carefully that placement is uniform. In the pentachord, make sure the vowels are radically distinct, without diphthong slurring from one to the other. Clarity and distinction of vowel itself is particularly "at home" with forward placement, and simply prompting the clarity of vowel will often bring the sound forward. The use of *nee*, while admirably bringing the sound forward, *may* have a tendency to tighten the sound as well. Softer dynamics and exercises that relax and loosen—vocal slides, for instance—are advantageous in combination with the above exercises. Similarly, the emphasis on vowel clarity and distinction can, at least in early stages of development, produce an unattractively choppy effect in getting from one vowel to the other. Relaxation of the air flow and concentration on the continuity of air is beneficial here.

Exercise 2

Sing any passage in your repertory on the textual vowels only, striving for distinction and purity of vowel. Then repeat the passage with *n* prefacing each of the vowels to bring the sound forward. In a third repetition, delete the *n*, but retain the placement it encourages.

(2) Timbral Diversity

The architecture of various pieces may well require individual lines to become prominent, as for example is common in cantus firmus textures. One's first inclination, I suspect, is to bring such lines out with dynamic contrast. And effective though that may be in many contexts, other approaches, such as the use of enhanced timbral differences, can help achieve the same thing. In rehearsal, for example, have the prominent line sung on *nee* with the other parts on *nah* to underscore the hierarchy of lines. Similarly, as a way of sensitizing singers to the architecture of imitative constructions, it is helpful to rehearse in a like way: Have all the singers sing on *ah*, except those with the imitative motive; those with the imitative motive render their lines on *nee*, rendering the architecture clear and nurturing the singers' awareness of their lines' relationship to the architectural whole.

(3) Controlling the Vibrato

In dealing with vibrato, the attempt to develop control and flexibility may prove more fruitful than total elimination, for too quick an attempt at elimination can lead to unattractive, forced singing. However, with flexibility and control, straight-tone singing becomes more simply one of many options at the singers' command. To nurture this, ask the singers to sing a sustained note with whatever they think a "moderate" vibrato might be. Call that "three on a scale of one to five." With the same sustained tone gradually manipulate the amount of vibrato: 3, 4, 2, 5, 1, 0 or 3, 4, 5, 4, 3, 2, 1, 0.

NOTES

1. *Ulysses* (New York: Vintage Books, 1961), 278.

2. Cf. for instance Gioseffo Zarlino's advocacy of a full voice in church, but a lower and gentler voice in private rooms. See Richard Wistreich, "Reconstructing Pre-Romantic Singing Technique," in John Potter, *The Cambridge Companion to Singing* (Cambridge: Cambridge University Press, 2000), 181.

3. "The Old Italian Organ and Its Music," *Diapason* 57, no. 2 (1966): 14, quoted in Jeffrey Kurtzman, *The Monteverdi Vespers of 1610: Music, Context, Performance* (Oxford: Oxford University Press, 1999), 360.

4. In Bernhard Ulrich, *Concerning the Principles of Voice Training during the A Cappella Period and until the Beginning of Opera (1474–1640)*, trans. John W. Seale (Minneapolis, Minn.: Pro Musica Press, 1973), 110. Cf. also Conrad von Zabern (1474) on the *vox trivaria* in Joseph Dyer, "The Voice in the Middle Ages," in Potter, *Companion*, 169–70 or Joseph Dyer, "Conrad von Zabern. Singing with Proper Refinement: *De Modo bene cantandi* (1474)," *Early Music* 6 (1978): 217: "[W]hosoever wishes to sing well and clearly must employ his voice in three ways: resonantly and trumpet-like for low notes, moderately in the middle range and more delicately for the higher notes—the more so the higher one ascends." Conrad's treatise is addressed to singers of liturgical chant.

5. On the importance of variety, one early and compelling voice is Guido of Arezzo, who in his *Micrologus* observes, "Nor is it strange that the hearing is pleased by a variety of sounds, since the sight rejoices in a variety of colors, the smell is fostered by a variety of odors, and the tongue enjoys tastes which change. For thus through the windows of the body the sweetness of suitable substances penetrates, in a marvelous manner, the inner chambers of the heart. This is the reason why with certain tastes and smells or even the contemplation of colors, the health just as much of the soul as of the body either diminishes or increases." In Marilyn Elizabeth Feller Somville, "Vowels and Consonants as Factors in Early Singing Style and Technique" (Ph.D. diss., Stanford University, 1967), 66. For an English translation of Guido's treatise, see *Hucbald, Guido, and John on Music: Three Medieval Treatises*, trans. Warren Babb (New Haven, Conn.: Yale University Press, 1978).

6. Quoted in Dyer, "The Voice in the Middle Ages," 174.

7. See Paschal P. Parente, "The Canticle of Canticles in Mystical Theology," *Catholic Biblical Quarterly* 6 (1944): 146. For an examination of musical settings of the *Song of Songs*, see Steven Plank, "Music of the Ravish'd Soul," *Musical Times* (1995): 466–71.

8. The principle is affirmed by such writers as Zarlino, Zacconi, and Cesare Crivellati. See Kurtzman, *Monteverdi Vespers*, 395. Interestingly, how-

ever, the necessity of meeting the acoustic challenge of large ecclesiastical buildings is countered by several points. One would be the secondary nature of "audience" in liturgical contexts. While some liturgical contexts do suggest performance for others, that is, for auditors, many equally suggest that liturgical singing was an action unto itself, and here the size of the building would not be critical. Moreover, even in large ecclesiastical buildings, the architectural choir forms a smaller, sometimes even an intimate, space in which to sing. Finally, as William Mahrt has suggested, the requirements of monastic singing—many hours a day—suggest a lightness rather than a fullness to save the voice. See "Chant," in *A Performer's Guide to Medieval Music,* ed. Ross W. Duffin (Bloomington: Indiana University Press, 2000), 16. Context is again the critical point, and one might well need to make the distinctions between chant and polyphony, on the one hand, and "concert" liturgies and "communal" liturgies on the other.

9. "The Canterbury Tales," in *The Works of Geoffrey Chaucer,* ed. F. N. Robinson (Boston: Houghton Mifflin, 1961), 18, ll. 122–23.

10. "Vocal Colour in English Sixteenth-Century Polyphony," *Journal of the Plainsong & Mediaeval Music Society* 2 (1979): 29.

11. I am grateful to Professor Robert Longsworth of Oberlin for sharing his thoughts on this issue. Descriptions of the Prioresse are from the "General Prologue," *Works of Geoffrey Chaucer,* 18, ll. 118–62.

12. In David Hiley, "Chant," in *Performance Practice: Music before 1600,* ed. Howard Mayer Brown and Stanley Sadie (New York: W. W. Norton, 1990), 44.

13. *Libellus de rudimentis musices* (1529). See Don Harrán, "Directions to Singers in Writings of the Early Renaissance," *Revue Belge de Musicologie* 41 (1987): 58.

14. Somville, "Vowels and Consonants," 75. See also Oliver Strunk, *Source Readings in Music History* (New York: W. W. Norton, 1950), 96.

15. For a discussion of Tinctoris and sweetness, see Rob Wegman, "Sense and Sensibility in Late-Medieval Music," *Early Music* 23 (1995): 299–312.

16. VI, 2 Prop V, p. 354. Quoted in Somville, "Vowels and Consonants," 111.

17. See Ravens, "A Sweet Shrill Voice: The Countertenor and Vocal Scoring in Tudor England," *Early Music* 26 (1998): 127.

18. Cf. Peter Phillips's interviews with English cathedral musicians. Discussing blend, Edward Higginbottom noted: "The blending problem is not caused by mixing young with old but rather with a certain timbre in different voices, which has less to do with age than with a type of vocal production. It can be overcome largely by getting everyone to sing at the same apparent dynamic level." Or from John Birch: "We are perhaps the smallest cathedral choir and we have to work hard at developing a new dynamic level below the ordinary softest one in order to achieve any blend." "The Golden Age Regained," *Early Music* 8 (1980): 6, 15.

19. For example, Cornish's Magnificat in the eighth tone and Sheppard's Magnificat in the first tone. See Wulstan, "Vocal Colour," 58. He further observes that the disposition of choirs in fifteenth- and sixteenth-century England rarely found more boys in the choir than men, suggesting that timbre would have played an important part in achieving balance. Cf. also Heinrich Finck's observation that trebles need to sing with a "certain fullness" of tone to achieve balance with the adult men singers. In Ulrich, *Principles*, 94.

20. Timothy McGee, in *Singing Early Music* (Bloomington: Indiana University Press, 1996), also notes that "when period pronunciations are substituted for modern pronunciations, poetic lines will often have both a different metric flow and a different set of rhymes, aspects that greatly change the sound properties of the musical line" (xi). McGee's wonderful resource offers pronunciation guides to vernaculars and vernacular Latins from Britain, France, Iberia, Italy, Germany, and the Low Countries. Especially valuable are the phonetic transcriptions of illustrative examples and an accompanying CD. Other works on the subject of historical pronunciation include Alison Wray, "The Sound of Latin in England before and after the Reformation," in *English Choral Practice 1400–1650* (Cambridge: Cambridge University Press, 1995), 74–89 and "English Pronunciation," 90–108. See also Ross W. Duffin, "National Pronunciation of Latin ca. 1490–1600," *Journal of Musicology* 4 (1985–1986): 217–26.

21. "The Solo Voice," in *A Performer's Guide to Renaissance Music*, ed. Jeffery T. Kite-Powell (New York: Schirmer, 1994), 5.

22. Cf. Frederick Gable: "The extent to which vibrato is employed and its size and speed can so obscure other elements of a performance that our very perception of a work can change simply on this basis." In "Some Observations Concerning Baroque and Modern Vibrato," *Performance Practice Review* 5 (1992): 90.

23. See Potter, *Companion*, 175.

24. See Kurtzman, *Monteverdi Vespers*, 361.

25. In Kurtzman, *Monteverdi Vespers*, 388. See also Carol MacClintock, *Readings in the History of Music in Performance* (Bloomington: Indiana University Press, 1979), 73.

26. Age, however, may be a mitigating factor. Peter Phillips's interviews with English cathedral organists associates a trend toward younger lay clerks with the hope of eliminating vibrato. On this point, Richard Seal was unequivocal: "Without a shadow of doubt vibrato comes with age, voices get looser, lose focus. Young people are more flexible, more malleable, the sound may not be so fulsome, but you can get further with it." In Phillips, "The Golden Age," 6. The observation is also historical. Christoph Bernhard in *Von der Singkunst* . . . (1650) noted that the tremulo was a problem with older singers. See Kurtzman, *Monteverdi Vespers*, 391, and Sally Allis Sanford, "Seventeenth- and Eighteenth-Century Vocal Style and Technique" (DMA diss., Stanford University, 1979), 71–72. Memorable is his instruction:

"If anyone would demand further evidence of the undesirability of the *tremulo,* let him listen to such an old man employing it while singing alone. Then he will be able to judge why the *tremulo* is [not] used by the most polished singers, except in *ardire."* Ibid.

27. "Singing Early Music," *Early Music* 4 (1976): 12. On the question of naturalness, cf. Mozart's letter to his father about the singer Meissner: "The human voice trembles naturally—but in its own way—and only to such a degree that the effect is beautiful. Such is the nature of the voice. . . . But the moment the proper limit is overstepped, it is no longer beautiful—because it is contrary to nature." In *The Letters of Mozart and His Family,* trans. Emily Anderson (New York: W. W. Norton, 1989), 552.

28. VI, 2, Prop. V, p. 353. In Somville, "Vowels and Consonants," 110–11. Emphasis added.

29. *Syntagma Musicum* III (1619), in MacClintock, *Readings,* 164.

30. See Kurtzman, *Monteverdi Vespers,* 391.

31. See Sanford, "Vocal Style and Technique," 8–9.

32. *Practica musicae* (1496), quoted in Alexander Blachly, "On Singing and the Vocal Ensemble I" in Kite-Powell, *A Performer's Guide,* p. 15.

33. "Scholarship & Performance: Peter Phillips Interviews Bruno Turner," *Early Music* 6 (1978): 203.

34. Cf. Frederick Gable's response to "pro-vibratoists" in which he tellingly reminds that "nobody complains about the straight tone of a piano." "Baroque and Modern Vibrato," 97–99.

35. For discussion, see Sanford in Kurtzman, *Monteverdi Vespers,* 393–94; see also Sanford, "A Comparison of French and Italian Singing in the Seventeenth Century," *Journal of Seventeenth-Century Music* 1, no. 1 (1995), available at www.sscm-jscm.org/jscm.

36. In Ulrich, *Principles,* 60. By way of contrast, Maffei's likening of the voice singing *gorgia* to a bagpipe is curious, for it suggests a "high intensity." See Somville, "Vowels and Consonants," 102.

37. No admonition is more amusing perhaps than that of Daniel Friderici in his *Musica figualis* (1618): "The cause of music is not served by boys who shout and yell so that their faces turn as dark red as a turkey cock, who open their mouths so wide that a carload of hay could be driven in." Ulrich, *Principles,* 71.

38. Richard Miller suggests this as early as 1832 and cites as well a paper by Garcia given to the Academy of Science in 1841 in which he advocated the technique to certain ends. See *English, French, German and Italian Techniques of Singing* (Metuchen, N.J.: Scarecrow Press, 1977), 86.

39. Conversely, raising the chin will elevate the larynx, though care should be taken that this does not produce a tension in the throat and neck.

40. I follow John Potter's *Vocal Authority: Singing Style and Ideology* (Cambridge: Cambridge University Press, 1998), 53.

Chapter 3

The Ensemble

The sound of early music ensemble singing and the ease with which interpretative goals are met are profoundly shaped by the makeup of the ensemble. How many singers? What kind of singers—on the treble parts, for instance, does one use boys, male falsettists, women, or some mixture of these? Do they sing with or without *colla parte* instrumentation? And with a bit of metaphorical license, we might also consider the physical setting in which the music is made a part of the ensemble itself, contributing its own qualities to the sound and its own aesthetic presence to the overall interpretation.[1]

It is a familiar notion that these things matter, and Romantic blindness to them has appeared in the cross-hairs of performance practice scholars often enough that performances by oversized ensembles are today relatively rare. Early comment on these matters could be pointed, as this excerpt from a report about a Leeds Festival performance of Palestrina in 1901 shows. In the report, the size of the ensemble and the costume of the singers, as well as their venue, are all taken to task:

> We were then carried back to the *sixteenth* century! by the strains of Palestrina. The introduction of the motet "Surge, illuminare," was an undoubted mistake. The motets of the great Italian master of church music need a much smaller choir, and one traditionally equipped, to do justice to that old-world and spiritual music; moreover, a town hall in broad daylight, with lady singers in festival attire, is not the proper environment for such devotional strains.[2]

Clearly in this case the end result was impeded by the forces assembled. The loss was a musical one, not a matter of historicism,
though surely a historical sense of things might well have led to
remedies that improved the aesthetic result. Accordingly, questions
of size, the use of instruments, vocal types, and physical setting are
investigated below toward that end.

SIZE

The size of historical ensembles can sometimes be shown with precision from pay-records and the like, though this can only take one
so far, for those types of sources do little to determine the utilization
of voices. In a chapel choir employing, say, ten singers, how many of
them sang in the rendition of four-part music? Manfred Bukofzer, in
his long-time classic essay, "The Beginnings of Choral Polyphony,"[3]
documents multiple singers on a single line in the early fifteenth
century, the establishment of a "chorus" as opposed to an ensemble
of soloists.[4] However, despite being able to document choral singing
at the beginning of the Renaissance, there is considerable evidence
that one- to-a-part singing—the ensemble of soloists—was frequent,
perhaps even normative in a number of contexts.[5] Contexts were, of
course, highly variable, and the solemnity of the occasion, the
venue, and patronal resources, might all well influence the composition of the ensemble.

Evidence regarding solo ensembles varies in its degree of concreteness. Moreover, the evidence can be adduced both pro and con-
tra. For example, in Rome Palestrina wrote the names of the eight
singers who would sing an eight-voice setting of the *Improperia* at
the Cappella Giulia, a clear indication of one-to-a-part.[6] Elsewhere
in Rome, at the German College in 1589 there is a reference to a
singer being unable to sing in chapel and sending a trombonist as
his substitute.[7] Why would a substitute be necessary in the first
place if more than one singer were singing a part? Moreover, that a
trombonist is sent rather than another singer adds further support:
The notes needed to be covered—by whomever! However, there is
documentary support for choral performance, as well. In 1630 papal
singers stated that three per part was necessary. In symmetry with
the discussion of Bach's choir and the evidence of his 1730 *Entwurff*,
one does not know whether this is an institutional minimum to

cover the exigencies of absence—this many singers in the choir will ensure that pieces can be sung one per part, even if absences occur—or whether it is an aesthetic desire for "choral" performance.[8] Moreover, references to the practice of giving a starting pitch in the sixteenth century—intoning the opening—are curious if the norm were solo singers. Given the frequency of imitative textures with one part beginning alone, in a solo ensemble presumably one would just begin.[9] In addition, one might also consider the frequency with which composers like Palestrina add an additional voice part in the final Agnus Dei section of mass settings. If the mass is performed by soloists, who sings the added part? Someone whose only assignment is that one final section? Thus, the evidence, at least here in a "snapshot" look at the Golden Age in Rome, seems to pull in both directions.

Some musical contexts were less ambiguous for soloists. Reduced textures, especially those bearing the labels indicating "trio," or "duo," seem not only well served by solo voices but true to their label when sung by soloists, although admittedly one should not press the literal meanings of such terms too far. In addition, polychoral pieces were often performed with one choir undoubled, providing a contrast both of volume and quality of sound. For example, in *Syntagma Musicum III*, Praetorius uses the words "omnes" and "solus" to designate numbers of performers on a part:

> In my *Concerti*, especially the Latin pieces but also in the German, where I do not use a *Chorus pro capellam*, for the most part I give the words *omnes* and *solus*, or voice, instrument, trombone, etc. Anyone can understand that and act accordingly. . . . Where *Voice* alone is found [as a part of the designation], the vocalist sings alone.[10]

Similarly, in his *Psalmen Davids* of 1619, Heinrich Schütz designates some of the choirs in polychoral textures as *cori favoriti*, composed of those whom the Chapelmaster "most favors." Though it is not explicit in his prefatory remarks, these *favoriti* have generally been interpreted as soloists. Schütz learned his polychoral writing in Venice under the guidance of Giovanni Gabrieli. Tellingly, in a work like Gabrieli's grandly polychoral motet "In ecclesiis," one choir is designated "voce" and given florid lines appropriate to solo singers.

It is not my point to rehearse all the evidence that pertains to one-per-part norms in the premodern era; rather, it is to underscore that

amid rival claims, this ensemble emerges as *at least* a common practice in music before the eighteenth century, and that this is an enor-
mous contrast—one that strikes at the very fundament of how we
define choirs—with modern choral practice. Modern choral practitioners may well, in this light, take advantage of the opportunity to
essay more passages with solo voices, especially in textures already
reduced. Few will renounce their choirs altogether! And so the question that emerges is, given our knowledge of the prominence of solo
ensembles, what does this mean for modern choirs?

- Heterogeneity of sound may be heightened
  Experience teaches that larger numbers of singers achieve a
  blend more quickly than do fewer singers on a part. Presumably, then, solo ensembles would have a qualitatively different ensemble sound than a blended choir, and the resulting
  heterogeneity may suggest a more colorful approach to
  choral timbre and to the distinction of individual lines.
- The volume of sound
  With a solo ensemble the total volume of sound may be objectively less than choral renditions, and this may tempt choir
  directors to favor more intimate levels of volume. Moreover,
  these intimate levels would certainly be within the capacity
  of solo ensembles. However, in a liturgical space, it seems
  more likely that the soloists themselves would favor loud
  singing (see chapter 2). In this case then, the historical spirit
  might be privileged and better served by full choral singing
  than by having a group sing with constraint in order to match
  a historical level of actual sound.
- Freedom of rendition
  Within the idiomatic bounds of the style, individual inflections of nuance and gesture might be given a heightened
  prominence, as might ornamentation. And while choral repli-
  cations of the gestures themselves might be difficult to
  achieve, making the music more gestural and nuanced itself
  is well within group capabilities.

Multiple singers on a part may well change the sound—the blend
is smoother and the fullness of texture is richer. However, I suspect
that the doubling of parts in the Renaissance did not radically alter
the volume, for choral ensembles were typically small, regardless of

the presence of doubling. This point is important to stress, for the question of "choral" versus "solo" becomes essentially then a qualitative one rather than a quantitative one grounded in dynamic level.

A number of studies have documented the size of various chapel choirs in the Renaissance[11] and the early Baroque. Drawing on them, we may note a range, the upper stratum of which may reflect the relationship between size and patronal magnificence, but certainly in the main, the choirs are small by modern standards. Moreover, noting the number of singers on a payroll—one of the principal types of supporting documents—is again no measure of the number of singers singing at one time.

Italian choirs around the turn of the sixteenth century seem to have experienced a time of growth. The cathedral at Milan went from seven adult singers in 1480 to fifteen in 1496; similarly the cathedral at Florence grew from five or six adults in 1480 to eighteen in 1493.[12] This level would be typical one hundred years later, as well. In 1603 Santa Maria Maggiore in Bergamo had eighteen singers (the disposition from treble to bass was 4, 5, 6, 2, with one singer unidentified as to part); in 1610 there were sixteen (2, 3, 5, 4, and two singers unidentified as to part).[13] This would also be the size of the Capella Giulia in the seventeenth century, though the Capella Sistina, reflecting perhaps its exclusive papal prestige and the magnificence attached to it, numbered thirty.[14] French and Lowland ensembles also experienced growth around the turn of the sixteenth century. For example, the twelve-man complement at places like the French Chapel Royal, Cambrai, and the Burgundian Chapel in the last part of the fifteenth century, would soon grow to sixteen, as at Cambrai in 1516 and Conde in 1523.[15]

These modest numbers, which again suggest total resources, not necessarily total number singing, are considerably overshadowed by the number of musicians under Lasso's direction at the Bavarian court chapel of Albrecht V in Munich. In 1570 he had sixty-two singers in the court chapel (sixteen boy trebles, six castrati, thirteen altos, fifteen tenors, and twelve basses). Moreover, they could be joined by instrumental forces that themselves numbered thirty.[16] In the context of the time it seems unusually lavish, and the extent of the personnel goes far beyond covering various absences and rotating duties, one feels sure. In a famous illumination by the Munich court painter, Hans Mielich, Lasso is depicted leading the court chapel.[17] The codex is lavish and its visual scale is matched by that of the suggested music-making. Over twenty singers (including three trebles) are deployed, for instance, joined by around fifteen instrumentalists (including violone, viole da braccio, transverse flute, curtal or bass recorder, cornett, rackett, and lute), with Lasso leading them all from the virginals. Certainly the texts of the penitential psalms do not invite this sort of elaborate style, and moreover, Lasso's style here is often austere. Yet the depiction shows rich grandeur of forces. One suspects it is a form of patronal showmanship rather than a performance norm that is depicted here, though the grand level of performance was clearly possible with the forces available. On the other hand, in that these vast numbers of performers are depicted with penitential psalms, not works of affective grandeur, this might argue for more frequent usage.

INSTRUMENTAL DOUBLING

The use of instruments to double or replace voice parts is a well-documented practice for sixteenth- and seventeenth-century music, though assessing the degree to which the practice was used is challenging and varies with context. In the modern revival of historic practices, *colla parte* voice doubling received considerable employment early on. Its usage was "historical," though one might suspect that its prominence was fueled in part by the desire to defamiliarize and set performances off from the a capella mainstream. Here was a way of dramatically going beyond the score—indicating to a listener that you had "historical" knowledge and that your performance made "historical claims"—and here was a way of borrowing the immediately visible historicity of period instruments. Again, support for the practice is strong, but motivations early in the historic performance revival may have been commercial as well as aesthetic. And this in turn may have given a skewed sense of how prevalent the practice in history really was.[18]

Certainly the aesthetic claims are strong ones, for the addition of instruments adds an important enrichment of color to the vocal timbre and enhances the presence of sound. With selective application, the use of instruments offers the means of highlighting or setting into relief certain sections where the text will benefit from such a gesture. And in the ornamental language of magnificence, the addition of instruments offers a highly affective vocabulary. Some have seen, as well, the use of instruments as an effective way of marking the structure of a piece—the prominent doubling of a cantus firmus line, for instance.[19] And to these aesthetic contributions, one must also add the sometime practical advantages of using instruments to shore up insecure lines, help secure intonation, and the like.[20]

The evidence in support of the practice of instrumental doubling varies. Iconography, for instance, shows numerous depictions of liturgical celebrations where both singers and instrumentalists are shown together at a time when voice doubling or substitution would have been the only possibility for their collaboration. For example, an often reproduced engraving by Adrian Collaert (*Encomium musices*, 1595) shows a pontifical mass in progress. A splendid image of a splendid occasion, the engraving shows the bishop as celebrant with deacon and subdeacon assisting with thurifer and taper bearers on the edge of the altar chapel. Behind this sizable group are the musicians—singers and instrumentalists (players of cornetts and trombones) all reading from a common lectern upon which a large-sized choirbook has been placed. Behind the altar on the Epistle (south) side is another group of musicians gathered around another common lectern. Though less clear in the engraving, one can see there a player of the cornett behind a singer. The context is clearly one of splendor, with the collaboration of instruments and voices combining to heighten that quality. The common lecterns—all read from the same page—as well as the style prevalent in the late sixteenth century strongly suggest that all the musicians were rendering the same parts.

The link of the practice to magnificence and splendor emerges in verbal description, as well. Royal attendance at chapel would often bring the accoutrements of royalty into the chapel, especially in the form of instrumental ensembles. Such occasions might also unsurprisingly be marked by the singing of particularly celebratory texts like the *Te Deum laudamus*. Thus we read of a 1525 liturgy at St. Paul's Cathedral in the presence of the king, where "the quere sang *Te Deum*, and the mynstrelles plaied on every side."[21] References like these, of course, do not pinpoint the nature of the collaboration. More clear in implication that the instruments and voices performed *together* are references like the following, describing Elizabeth I's visit to Christ Church Cathedral, Oxford, in 1566: "She entred into the church, and there abode while the quyer sang and play'd with cornetts, Te Deum."[22]

Certain composers were specific in their references to *colla parte* instrumentation. Both Schütz and Praetorius essayed large-scale polychoral compositions in the first part of the seventeenth century—pieces that gained some of their scale from the use of doubling instruments as well as innovative obbligato lines for instruments. Both composers address, in fact, the physical placement of the doubling instruments, advising that they be in a different place from the singers. This gains the twofold advantage of a broader dissemination of sound and supposedly also helps to keep the text clear.[23] Praetorius, for example, in the commentary to his *Polyhymnia Caduceatrix et Panegyrica,* observes that in "small churches and narrow chambers" one might best omit the strings so that the voices and their text will not be obscured or "one must (as is often chosen) have the instruments somewhat far away [from the voices]."[24] Or, for instance, with reference to his setting of "Wir glauben," he writes "In case [more] instruments are present, it is much nicer to hear those same [instruments] also used along with the voices, however, set a bit to the side."[25]

If the practice offered gains magnificence, practicality, and variety of color and expression, it is also problematic in some quarters. This is a very context-driven issue. At the Papal Chapel, for instance, the absence of instruments was traditional, and their absence furthered an aura of unadulterated purity, a musical halo to surround the pope's liturgy. (The aura of purity extended to social matters, as well, such as the prescribed unmarried state of the singers in the Capella Sistina, even though ordination was not mandated.) The attitude toward instruments in the premodern era was equivocal: decidedly mixed and variable. In part the conservative view would see them as tainted with secularity, stained by association with worldly licentiousness. This was a taint going back to antiquity, as the writings of Augustine of Hippo and St. John Chrysostom document. However, biblical associations were also strong, as in various psalmodic references—Psalm 150 is a classic example—and in references to the use of instruments in the rites of the Temple, such as I Chronicles 25: "They were all under the direction of their father in the house of the Lord with cymbals, harps, and lyres for the service of the house of God." Moreover, the permeable wall between church and state would often see the trappings of secular majesty easily appropriated into liturgy. Instruments, unsurprisingly, were often part of the trappings.

That *colla parte* doubling is generally unspecified in the musical sources, to say nothing of the absence of reference to specific instrumentation, should not lead to the conclusion that any instruments in any combination were used. The casual attitude of the day toward matters of instrumentation was bounded by idiom and convention, and these would fruitfully narrow the choices.[26] There is evidence to suggest that winds were preferred. Certainly their use of breath and vowel give them a vocality that worked especially well with vocal ensembles. And certain wind instruments, like the cornett, were particularly known for the congeniality of their tone color among voices. Marin Mersenne's famous description of cornetts in cathedrals is both poetically rich and exemplary: "As to the characteristic quality of sound that they produce, it is similar to the brilliance of a sun's ray, which appears in the shadow or the darkness, when one hears it among the voices in the cathedrals or chapels."[27] There is also at least one reference privileging winds on the basis of their stability of pitch. The Anglican priest and amateur musician Charles Butler opined in his *Principles of Musick* (1636) that "because Entata [strings] ar often out of tun; (which sometime happeneth in the mids of the Musik, when it is neither good to continue, nor to correct the fault) therefore, to avoid all offence (where the least shoolde not bee givn) in our Chyrch-solemnities only the Winde-instruments (whose Notes ar constant) bee in use."[28]

If winds were preferred, the most common wind ensemble for church music was the choir of trombones, joined by cornett as the treble voice. That this was a mixed consort instead of a full consort of trombones through all the ranges owes in part to the rarity and late appearance of the soprano trombone[29] and its problematic nature, namely that with an instrument that small, the slide positions become dangerously close one to another. But if the soprano trombone was problematic, the cornett proved ideal, for its chameleon-like tone has unusual blendability with treble voices, and the presence of vowel in its sound renders its tone distinctively human. We can sense the prominence of this ensemble with voices on a number of fronts. Iconography once again confirms their liturgical usage, as do pay records. Significantly, for instance, the instrumental ensemble established by Andrea Gabrieli at San Marco in Venice around 1568 was led by the great cornett virtuoso, Girolamo dalla Casa. Though independent instrumental pieces were part of the Venetian liturgical practice, there seems little doubt but that dalla

Casa's ensemble also provided instrumental support to the choir, *colla parte*. And that the association between the trombone choir and things ecclesiastical was a strong one is convincingly underscored in the emblematic scoring of Schütz's *Historia der Geburt Jesum Christi*. The various intermedii here present tableaux with different characters from the Christmas narrative, and the characters receive a measure of dramatic distinction by emblematic scoring. Thus, the shepherds are accompanied by rusticlike recorders, King Herod by a monarchical pairing of trumpet and cornett, etc. Significantly, the high priests of the temple are accompanied by a choir of trombones.[30]

In general, although voice doubling by trombones and cornetts was more a part of unwritten convention than notated practice, the convention itself has later notated echoes in the church music of Haydn, Mozart, and Beethoven. Masses by these three and their contemporaries often have alto, tenor, and bass trombone doubling the alto, tenor, and bass vocal lines in choral tuttis, notating what at one time would have been an unwritten assumption. That the soprano part curiously remains undoubled by a brass wind reflects the decline of the cornett in the nineteenth century.

One style of voice doubling that emerges around 1600 is the organ intabulation, wherein generally contrapuntal scores were sung to the accompaniment of a doubling keyboard.[31] (That it is the organ doing the doubling may perhaps trade on its sacred associations, but also, in that it is a wind instrument, albeit a mechanical one, it may also claim a degree of vocality in its sound production.) This practice was particularly associated with the contrapuntal *prima prattica* style in an age when this particular style was under attack from the humanistic avant-garde. The practice itself seems to offer, in part, a gratification of the taste for basso continuo that was emerging in other styles, and may trade on that fashionability. But it also seems an eminently practical and economic way of supplying the timbral enrichment that *colla parte* playing offered.

While in noncontrapuntal styles the fashion for basso continuo was eminently workable, in contrapuntal writing where linear integrity is critical, basso continuo risked obscuring the very elements at the heart of the composition. Hence the important distinction between a realization of implied harmonies from figures and the literal rendering of the individual lines and the advocacy of exact doubling for contrapuntal pieces. Even composers whom we particularly associate with the new style made the distinction. Schütz, for example, in a number of works was critical of the practice of continuo, and unsurprisingly, favoring linear integrity, advocated intabulation. One strong example would be the preface to the *Cantiones Sacrae* (1625): "I would beg the organists who wish to satisfy more sensitive ears, however, not to spare the pains of writing out all the parts in score or so-called tablature; should you wish to accompany, in the usual manner, solely from the [figured] continuo part, I should find it misguided and clumsy."[32] Lodovico da Viadana added similar support to tablature in his prefatory material to *Cento Concerti Ecclesiastici* (1602):

> No tablature has been made for these Concertos, not in order to escape the trouble, but to make them easier for the Organist to play, since, as a matter of fact, not everyone would play from tablature at sight, and the majority would play from the Partitura [i.e., the Organ Bass] as being less trouble; I hope that the Organists will be able to make the said tablature at their own convenience, which, to tell the truth, is much better.[33]

THE TYPE OF SINGERS

As we have seen, instruments doubling the voices contribute strongly to scale and color. Color, of course, is also richly determined by the types of voices used in the ensemble. Historically the premodern choir is most often an all-male one. Repertories not under ecclesiastical regulation and constraint, like the madrigal and the chanson, were certainly performed, though not exclusively, by mixed-gender ensembles, but these ensembles were most often groups of soloists. Choral performance is most often then tied to the church, and its views on mixed ensembles are long-standing and well-known. Fearing the female voice would become an element of enticement, seduction, and distraction, the church traditionally held to St. Paul's dictum, *mulieres in ecclesiis taceant.*[34] However, the all-male choir admits a number of possibilities, each with timbral distinction. The treble line was taken variously by boys, castrati,[35] or in some choirs, both together; possibly also by adult males singing falsetto.[36] The alto range was taken by adult males, either in falsetto, high tenors singing in "natural" voice, or perhaps a combination of the two; the modern continental practice of unchanged boys' voices singing the alto part does not appear to have been common historically, though it did exist.[37] The evidence of these configurations once again leads one away from a single interpretation of historical sound. Moreover, obviously with regard to the castrati, the ensemble is not reproducible, and equally obviously, the all-male ensemble will in some circumstances be unattainable or undesirable. However, much as the sound of a solo ensemble may be a guiding tenet rather than a threat to choirs, the modern mixed choir may also use the sounds of the all-male ensemble as a historical guide. What qualities arise? Lightness and purity from the boys, one suspects, though as the contrast of modern continental trebles with their English counterparts reveals, or even the contrast of different Cambridge choirs—the comparison of King's College and St. John's College can be dramatic—it would be a mistake to imagine that full-throated singing was neither attainable nor, to some tastes, desirable. Similarly, the modern Anglican falsettist tends to present a wafting, leanness of sound, but this could be more a matter of style than the nature of the voice itself. However, the wafting, relaxed sound seems to have a degree of historicity to it. For example, the English traveler Thomas Coryat (1577–1617) heard a falsettist and remarked on his sound, "Besides it was farre the more excellent, because it was nothing forced, strained, or affected, but came from him with the greatest facilitie that ever I heard."[38]

One important factor to keep in mind in adapting the historical all-male model to mixed voices is the question of "relative range." An "a" below middle "c"sung by a female alto will be low in her range and will often be loud and dark as a result; the same note sung by a male falsettist will be weak for its nearness to the break between head and chest voice; the same note sung by a high tenor will be effortless. Also, a high "d" in the treble staff will be effortless for a female soprano, though high for a male falsettist, who will likely use increased volume to help secure it. These issues of relative range focus on sound qualities associated with various strata of engendered voices. Accordingly, creative voice assignments may have a good effect. In the instance of the "a" below middle "c," it may make more sense to have female sopranos lightly sing it by analogy to a male falsettist's weak part of the range, than female altos, whose temptation to bring a robustness to that part of the range is dissonant with the historical model. Similarly, having female altos sing higher than usual may put them more on the same footing as males entering the higher parts of their range. This is not only because of the significant increase of volume that may accompany securing higher notes, but also because of the relative carrying power of certain parts of the register, regardless of how loudly they are sung. On the other hand, one may choose to make replicative dynamic adjustments to bring things closer in line to the historical model. Moreover, one might consider whether the dynamic exigencies of range are secondary concerns to the context of the pitches themselves. That is, the fact that a melody goes into the weak part of a falsettist's range might be disadvantageous to the musical context, and the female rendition sung in full voice becomes potentially an aesthetic advantage. However, this latter posture suggests a historical dissonance between means and ends that would seem unusual in an age of such high artistic accomplishment.

THE PHYSICAL SETTING

With a degree of metaphorical license, it is not too difficult to see the physical setting of the music-making as part of the performing forces, for it shapes the sound, enhances the reception, and inflects the interpretation—all tangible, critical parts of the performance itself—and it does these things often quite dramatically. It would be a vain task to try to generalize the historical venue for Renaissance choral music. Liturgical motets, as David Fallows reminds, were performed not only in liturgical spaces, but also *al fresco* or in banqueting halls, etc., for a variety of occasions.[39] And even assuming for the point of discussion that they were restricted to consecrated buildings, the consecrated buildings in use, say, in 1600 might have been gothic spaces, claiming four hundred years of continuous use, or they might have been fifty-year-old buildings in modern style; they may have been vast cathedral spaces, or they may have been intimate chapels; they might also have been relatively contained spaces within larger ones, in the way that the architectural choir of a church might, by virtue of the choir screen, have defined a self-contained space. Moreover, whatever the space, it may have been adapted with acoustic-altering material, such as banners and tapestries, etc. Thus, in this case, historical realities are much too variable to generalize in detail, but this should not blind us to the ways in which space is influential.

In an interview, the venerable David Willcocks, for instance, once noted the way in which the chapel at King's College, Cambridge, influenced the style of performance during his tenure there. He observed:

> [I]t [the chapel] narrows the range of expression because if you sing *ff* you will hear it five seconds later; if you reach *mf* at the climax you can move on to something else two seconds later. That restriction dictates the tone—semiquaver runs *have* to be light, detached and rather soft in order to achieve clarity.[40]

In Willcocks's example, it is the building as part of the acoustic phenomenon that is significant. And this is surely the most familiar way in which we talk about buildings and performance. The building restricts the dynamic range, requires more distinct articulation, requires slower tempos, etc. Certainly these have historical values; that is, it is safe to assume that performers have always been sensitive to these things. Accordingly, if we are guided by their example, we too will adopt a flexible attitude in response to the dictates of setting. However, amidst that flexibility, we may still want to be guided by the way in which original performance venues—even ones perhaps very different from our own—may have shaped interpretation. It is an interesting dynamic tension between what "works" in one modern setting—the practicalities—and how one understands what would have been practical in an original setting—practicalities that may be closely allied with composer intention. The difficulties of reconciling that tension are unsurprisingly one of the most compelling reasons for striving to match modern performance to historical setting.

As an example, we might consider Giovanni Gabrieli's well-known concertato motet, "In ecclesiis," written to be performed in the cavernous acoustic of the Basilica of St. Mark's in Venice. One of the most striking moments in the motet is the use of slow, homophonic block chords in harmonic third-relations on the repeated word, "Deus." (See ex. 3.1.) Homophonic haloes of names is not a new effect by any means, nor is it one that relies on a single acoustic for its effect. For dramatic rhetorical effect and in acknowledgment of the reverberant acoustic of the basilica, Gabrieli has written rests after the declamations. These necessary air-clearing pauses introduce perhaps an element of expectancy, well suited to the beseeching text lines that have immediately preceded. Libera nos, salva nos, vivifica nos (free us, save us, give us life) are all pleas, and the pauses after "Deus" can easily become like question marks, waiting for an answer: *Free us, save us, enliven us. God? God?* And this is heightened by the steady rise of the chromatic line without downward resolution. Many renditions of the passage have im-bued it with climactic drama, with each block chord growing into the other, maximizing the inherent tension in the chromatic line. And the result is an air of insistence: *God! God!* However, in the original acoustic the chromatic line might well be obscured with-out an element of dynamic taper before arriving at the next chro-matic note, and it does not seem a stretch to imagine that Gabrieli, knowing that particular acoustic intimately, may have had some-thing like that in mind. From the standpoint of interpretation this offers an expressive gesture that might not have arisen in a drier acoustic, and more important it is one that undercuts the insistent tone, replacing it with something that embodies perhaps the need for the plea in the first place. Thus, even if we are well aware that flexibility in our response to acoustics is warranted on historical and other grounds, a consideration of the original acoustic and its implications for interpretation remains an important considera-tion.

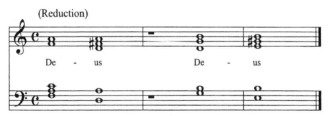

Example 3.1.   Giovanni Gabrieli, "In ecclesiis" (*Symphoniae sacrae*, 1615)

Influential elements of setting may also well include the configu-ration of singers within the space. We know that this was sometimes of specific concern, as for instance the 1564 action of the maestro of the Capella Sistina to restore the choir's traditional way of standing around the lectern: "Formerly, when music was sung, the singers, as the dean requested, stood in front of the lectern in this way: sopra-nos on the left and contraltos on the right of the lectern, and tenors on the left at the back of the sopranos and basses on the right at the back of the contraltos."[41] The aural effects of this reconfiguration are unclear, but it is safe to conclude they were distinctive enough to warrant the action. In addition, the implications of singing from a common lectern itself are several. Most especially it underscores a truly ensemble ethos in which all are focused—harmonized—in one action; it positions singers in a way that enhances the act of singing as an aural action, rather than a visual one, for the very situation of *not* holding something to look at seems to free one from the fetters of looking, and it also radically changes the status of any who are there as "conductors," for they, too, are looking at the same lectern. Thus, they come *from* the group rather than as an outsider to it, and so positioned, they command less attention.

Configuration may also reflect architectural style, and this may be exploited in the construction of the music as well. A clear case in point is the divided choir that places equal and complete forces on each side of the choir, facing each other. The sides are traditionally named "Decani" and "Cantoris," referring to the side on which the dean has his stall and the side on which the precentor has his, south and north respectively. This division is most likely rooted in the antiphonal performance of psalms, but by the sixteenth century in England, polyphony exploited subdivisions of the choir for spatial and textural effect.

So far we have discussed physical setting only insofar as it has influence on the acoustic property of the performance, only so far as it becomes an element of the sound. But, much as a frame can inflect the meaning of a picture, and much as the room in which we hang a painting can radically shape our sense of the image, so too does the visual element of the performing space become an important part of the performance itself.[42] A motet performed in a devotional space, regardless of whether it is being performed with devotional intent by the devout for the devout, will capture to a degree something of the interaction of the visual and sonic worlds that would have characterized its "historic" performance. In situ, a crucifix will underscore central tenets behind the motet's text; the translucent walls of stained glass will create a distinctive aura around the space that suggests the otherness of the holy; candlelight will render the space mysterious, etc. And going beyond the realm of the visual, the lingering smell of incense recalls to mind the prayers of those in that place. These elements then comprise a frame for the motet that was much a part of its historical fabric. And if the modern performer is concerned with interpreting the historic work, then the fabric will need to be considered as a seamless weave.

Admittedly, there is a world of difference between a modern performance of Renaissance motets in a church, a concert of the motets in a church with a faux liturgical context, and a use of the motets in actual liturgy. This is not to privilege one over the other, but rather to affirm that the visual setting in all of these is interactive with the music and with the audience, and as that was so historically, so too might it be a thoughtful part of a "historical" performance. *All* visual settings, of course, will be interactive with the music and with the audience—a concert stage, overstuffed auditorium seats, and tuxedos no less than an altar chapel, wooden pews, and cassocks. And one might argue that the former will offer in its eclecticism a contrasting frame that allows us to see and hear the motet in new and interesting ways. That, of course, is an interpretative choice. But is it an interpretative choice between equals? To the degree that the original physical setting was influential in the shaping of the musical event, to the degree that the music was part of an integrated "multimedia" presentation, I would suggest that the answer is "no."

In advancing claims that historical performance might be both visual as well as sonic, I am mindful that those claims may lead to exaggerations. There *is* a dissonance in singing a Renaissance motet in the formal attire that arose in the late nineteenth century to an audience no longer bound by that dress code, in a modernist hall.[43] But that dissonance (again, potentially a creative one) should not lead us to believe that historical performance must be a game of costume dress-up. Again, the critical point seems to be the degree to which the context has been determinative of the aesthetic substance that one is interpreting. This is certainly the compelling point behind Peter Kivy's caution that we separate aesthetic concerns from archaeological ones in these matters. He writes:

> I can give a plausible story about how the structure of the coronation Mass and its shining musical surface have been aesthetically fashioned for ceremonial performance in a place of worship of a certain kind. I can give no such plausible story of how the Brandenburg Concertos were musically fashioned for musicians wearing wigs. They could be wearing bowler hats or baseball caps for all that it matters aesthetically.[44]

In other words, to the degree that setting was historically influential on the aesthetic substance of a work, to that degree setting needs to be both a subject for interpretation and a metaphorical but vital member of the performing ensemble.

NOTES

1. Cf. John Potter, *The Cambridge Companion to Singing* (Cambridge: Cambridge University Press, 2000), 159: "Think of the building . . . as an extension of the ensemble. The acoustic acts as both amplifier and speaker, and you should feel that you are singing the whole building."

2. *Musical Times* 42 (1901): 733, quoted in *Early Music* 13 (1985): 71.

3. In *Studies in Medieval and Renaissance Music* (New York: W. W. Norton, 1950), 176–89.

4. In this light, the increasing size of choirbooks in the latter part of the century is suggestive that, at least in certain contexts, the idea took hold. "The size of the staves varies between one and two inches, the size of the whole page between 20x14 and 28x19 inches." Bukofzer, "The Beginnings of Choral Polyphony," 181.

5. With regard to the sixteenth and seventeenth century, see, inter alia, Richard Sherr, "Performance Practice in the Papal Chapel during the 16th Century," *Early Music* 15 (1987): 453–62; and Jean Lionnet, "Performance Practice in the Papal Chapel during the 17th Century," *Early Music* 15 (1987): 3–15: "Modern choral practice—many singers to each part—did not start before the final years of the 17th century; only then do we begin to find any indications of the use of ripieno singers, and it seems that this practice became general there only during the second half of the 18th century" (12). Graham Dixon offers a cautionary note, however about Lionnet's conclusions: "Responses to his ideas note that many of his references are to Crucifixus . . . and Holy Week . . . , both of which might characteristically use single voices without any implication that that was true for the rest of the repertory." "The Performance of Palestrina," *Early Music* 22 (1994): 72–73. With regard to the eighteenth century, the writings of Joshua Rifkin and, recently, Andrew Parrott's *The Essential Bach Choir* (New York: Boydell Press, 2000), are fundamental.

6. Sherr, "Papal Chapel," 457.

7. Dixon, "Performance of Palestrina," 670.

8. Sherr, "Papal Chapel," 458. For the text and translation of the Bach *Entwurff*, see Parrott, *The Essential Bach Choir*, inter alia.

9. Sherr, "Papal Chapel," 456.

10. In Carol MacClintock, *Readings in the History of Music in Performance* (Bloomington: Indiana University Press, 1979), 144.

11. See, for example, Frank D'Accone, "The Performance of Sacred Music in Italy during Josquin's Time, c. 1475–1525," in *Proceedings of the International Josquin Festival Conference* (1971), ed. Edward E. Lowinsky (Oxford: Oxford University Press, 1976). D'Accone's data support a view of larger chapels between 1430 and 1480 having one or two singers on lower parts, with more on the treble line (for balance), though the Capella Sistina or courts such as Ferrara would have had considerably larger numbers.

12. See Christopher Reynolds, "Sacred Polyphony," in *Performance Practice: Music before 1600,* ed. Howard Mayer Brown and Stanley Sadie (New York: W. W. Norton, 1990), 188.

13. Jerome Roche, cited in Jeffrey Kurtzman, *The Monteverdi Vespers of 1610: Music, Context, Performance* (Oxford: Oxford University Press, 1999), 380.

14. Dixon, "The Performance of Palestrina," 669. Dixon also notes that lesser institutions at the time, like Santa Maria in Trastevere, maintained a modest complement of eight voices.

15. David Fallows, "The Performing Ensembles in Josquin's Sacred Music," *Tijdschrift van de Vereniging voor Nederlandse Muziekgeschiedenis* 35, nos. 1/2 (1985): 39.

16. Reynolds, "Sacred Polyphony," 188.

17. Mielen Codex (D Mbs Mus Ms A II). The illumination is reproduced in color in *Die Musik in Geschichte und Gegenwart* (1960 ed.), s.v. "Lasso."

18. Kenneth Kreitner describes the move away from frequent voice doubling since the late 1970s in "Bad News or Not? Thoughts on Renaissance Performance Practice," *Early Music* 26 (1998): 323–25. He further articulates the view that unaccompanied choral renditions represent the ideal for sacred polyphony to ca. 1600.

19. Though at one time a popular practice in modern performances of older repertories, this hierarchical use of scoring has waned. David Fallows observes, "Hypotheses [of instrumental use] related to analytical scoring, that is, scoring that attempts to separate one voice from the texture, are surely misguided. What evidence there is would seem to suggest that instrumental participation, favored for certain magnificent purposes, took the form of doubling and had no more sophisticated musical intent." Fallows, "Performing Ensembles," 38. For a contrary view, see Wilhelm Ehmann's "Was gut auf Posaunen ist, etc.," *Zeitschrift für Musikwissenschaft* 17 (1935): 171–75, in which certain sixteenth-century motets are singled out for instrumental doubling by trombones by virtue of cantus firmus lines.

20. Cf. the observations of an anonymous Englishman who notes that instruments were useful for keeping "all the voices in tyme and in tune together, so that by listening to the organ, every of the singers may correct his owne error, either for ill tuninge of the songe or for ill timinge." GB lbm Roy 18 B 19, quoted in Andrew Parrott, "Grett and Solompne Singing: Instruments in English Church Music before the Civil War," *Early Music* 6 (1978): 184–85.

21. Cited in Parrott, "Grett and Solompne Singing," 183.

22. Parrott, "Grett and Solompne Singing," 183.

23. See Frederick Gable, "St. Gertrude's Chapel, Hamburg, and the Performance of Polychoral Music," *Early Music* 15 (1987): 237.

24. Margaret Anne Boudreaux, "Michael Praetorius;' 'Polyhymnia caduceatrix et panegyrica' (1619): An Annotated Translation" (DMA diss., University of Colorado, Boulder, 1989), 77. Distance was not always sought, however. Praetorius also notes that, "[It is good to] have an instrumentalist right next to the boys as is customary in the schools. Then the untrained boy can sing the unembellished [line] and the instrumentalist can play the diminutions." Ibid., 103.

25. Boudreaux, "Praetorius," 149.

26. For an exhaustive treatment of early seventeenth-century choices after the Italian style, see Praetorius, *Syntagma Musicum*, III.

27. Marin Mersenne, *Harmonie Universelle: The Books on Instruments*, trans. Roger E. Chapman (The Hague: Martinus Nijhoff, 1957), 345.

28. Quoted in Parrott, "Grett and Solompne Singing," 186.

29. The earliest surviving soprano trombone dates only from 1677; the instrument itself appears to have developed in the last part of the seventeenth century. See Howard Weiner, "The Soprano Trombone Hoax," *Historic Brass Society Journal* 13 (2001): 138–60.

30. Schütz also adopts the trombones for King David in his lament "Fili mi, Absalon" from the *Symphoniae Sacrae I.*

31. For discussion, see Gregory S. Johnston, "Polyphonic Keyboard Accompaniment in the Early Baroque: An Alternative to Basso Continuo," *Early Music* 26 (1998): 51–64. See also Dixon, "Performance of Palestrina." Girolamo Diruta was explicit in his support of the practice in his second volume of *Il transilvano* (1609). For an English translation, see *The Transylvanian*, trans. Murray C. Bradshaw and Edward J. Soehnlen (Henryville, Pa.: Institute of Mediaeval Music, 1984).

32. In Johnston, "Polyphonic Keyboard Accompaniments," 56.

33. In F. T. Arnold, *The Art of Accompaniment from a Thoroughbass as Practiced in the XVIIth & XVIIIth Centuries* (New York: Dover, 1965), vol. 1, 14–15.

34. I Cor. 14: 34. Tresses were also troublesome; hence the long tradition of hats and scarves worn in church by women, avoiding the issue of bareheadedness. The vocal tradition persisted in both Reformed and Roman churches until well into the eighteenth century. In the Roman Church, it was not unusual until the Second Vatican Council. The most tenacious adherents to the tradition—now on aesthetic, rather than moral grounds, however—are the Anglican cathedrals and the collegiate chapel choirs of Oxford and Cambridge Universities. However, the recent advent of girl choristers at several English cathedrals, including Salisbury and Wells, is a notable and unsurprisingly contentious innovation.

35. On the history of the castrati, see, inter alia, Angus Heriot, *The Castrati in Opera* (London: Secker and Warburg, 1956; reprint, 1975); and John Rosselli, "The Castrati as a Professional Group and a Social Phenomenon, 1550–1850," *Acta Musicologica* 60 (1988): 143–79.

36. For a history of the male alto, see Peter Giles, *The History and Technique of the Countertenor* (Aldershot, England: Scolar Press, 1994); Ardran and Wulstan, "The Alto or Countertenor Voice," *Music & Letters*, 48 (1967): 17–22; Robert Garreton, "The Falsettists," *Choral Journal*, 24, no. 1 (1983): 5–7; Frederic Hodgson, "The Contemporary Alto," *Musical Times*, 106 (1965): 293–94; Frederic Hodgson, "The Countertenor," *Musical Times*, 106 (1965): 216–17; and Roland Tatnell, "Falsetto Practice: A Brief Survey," *The Consort*, 22 (1965): 31–35.

37. Roger Bowers cites several examples in five-part sixteenth-century liturgical contexts in England. See "To Chorus from Quartet: The Performing Resource for English Church Polyphony, c. 1390–1559," in *English Choral Practice 1400–1650* (Cambridge: Cambridge University Press, 1995), 35.

38. Quoted in Ravens, "A Sweet Shrill Voice: The Countertenor and Vocal Scoring in Tudor England," *Early Music* 26 (1998): 127. Coryat traveled in western Europe in 1608, recording his observations in *Coryat's Crudities* and *Coryat's Cramb*.

39. Fallows, "Performing Ensembles," 32.

40. In Peter Phillips, "The Golden Age Regained 2," *Early Music* 8 (1980): 181. Presumably the converse might be asserted as well, namely that a dead building requires a greater range of dynamic.

41. Sherr, "Papal Chapel," 453. Nota bene: This arrangement reflects the typical layout of the individual voice parts on the folio.

42. For discussion of the way in which context becomes a determiner of meaning, see the classic essay by Walter Benjamin, "The Work of Art in an Age of Mechanical Reproduction," in *Illuminations* (London: Fontana, 1992) and the compelling study by John Berger, *Ways of Seeing* (New York: Penguin, 1977).

43. Perhaps the biggest dissonance of all is that of a liturgical repertory in a public concert.

44. In *Authenticities*, 102–3.

Chapter 4

What Pitches
Shall We Sing?

PITCH STANDARDS AND TRANSPOSITION

For those whose musical experiences have been largely formal and in mainstream repertories, the very idea that "what pitches shall we sing?" is a question at all will seem alien. Allegiance to a detailed, exact score that specifies all aspects of the sound with precision has long been characteristic of many forms of modern music-making, and, in fact, the degree of allegiance has in some ways become the benchmark of artistic integrity. However, a foray into vernacular traditions shows how familiar the idea of coexistent multiple versions of pieces can be, and how uncontroversial procedures like transposition seem. The popular singer who says to her accompanist, "I think tonight we'd best do this down in B-flat," will get no raised eyebrow from accompanist nor listener. However, the conductor who announces to her assembled orchestra that the horn players have all had the flu this past week, so *Eroica* will be taken down a step or two, exists only in horn players' dreams.

The flexibility of the popular singer brings us closer to certain premodern attitudes about pitch standards and their place in the relationship between performer and composer. For the pop singer in our scenario, "Stormy Weather" remains "Stormy Weather," whether in B-flat, D, or F. (*Eroica* in C, however, becomes, at best, a gloss on Beethoven's work.) The pop singer indulges personal comfort of range to offer the song in that place that is most natural and expressive. And indeed, much in the Renaissance view supports a similar perspective, viz., that the performer, regardless of the implied pitch

level of the notation, should feel free to place it where it is natural
and easy.

Heinrich Finck, for instance, in his *Practica Musica* notes that:

[L]est one voice blunt or disturb another by its own sound, it should be
seen to that the discantus and the alto not rise higher than they should,
or that no singer strains his voice; for many singers change their tone
colors, becoming black in the face and come to the end of their breath.
I myself have seen with indignation excellent singers become debased
and deformed, with distorted and gaping mouths, with head tossed
back, and with bleating and barbaraic cries, which (with preconceived
opinion) they hold bellowing and singing to be one and the same
thing, they ruin and deform the most beautiful music. What a de-
plorable sight![1]

Variations on this same theme are voiced by Jerome of Moravia: "To
start the song too low is called howling, too high is called shouting.
To begin in the middle voice is called singing."[2]

Did such performer flexibility challenge compositional auton-
omy? In general, this would seem unlikely. Given, for instance, the
degree to which composers were also often the performers of their
own works, the paradigm of flexibility would perhaps have been
deeply entrenched. And even in the compositional record of things,
a strong sense of fixed pitch is easily challenged, as we see, for instance, in comparing the sources for Adrian Willaert's Pentecost
motet, "Veni Sancte Spiritus." As Alejandro Planchart notes, the 1545
print and the manuscript version in the Medici Codex differ by a
fourth.[3] Was this revised "aesthetic" thinking on Willaert's part or a
casual attitude toward pitch level rooted in local circumstance? The
latter seems more likely, but in any case, the evidence suggests that
the nature of the work itself is not specific to any one pitch level.

This prevailing attitude may derive from the performance practice
of plainsong. William Mahrt, in a thoughtful discussion of the issue,
reminds that even though the typical range for a mode is around an
octave, the cumulative range of all the modes together doubles that.
Yet, sung by the same choir, it would seem "inconceivable that one
chant should be sung an octave higher than another." One more
readily believes that the range of the choir was more uniform—like
its personnel—and that notated pitch was not a guide to pitch level.
Mahrt then makes the leap to polyphonic implications. If the
polyphony is an elaboration of the chant, as in a cantus firmus com-

position, then it probably is an elaboration of the chant *where sung*, not where written, implying a free approach to polyphonic transposition, too.[4]

Certainly the comfort of moderate range encourages naturalness, akin surely to the cultivated appearance of grace enshrined in works like Castiglione's famous *The Courtier,* and its nurture of *sprezzatura.* In Book I he records:

> But I, imagining with my selfe often times how this grace commeth, leaving apart such as have it from above, finde one rule that is most generall which in this part (me thinke) taketh place in all things belonging to a man in worde or deede, above all other. And that is to eschue as much as a man may, and as a sharpe and daungerous rock, too much curiousness, and (to speake a new word) to use in everye thing a certain disgracing, to cover arte withall, and seeme whatsoever he doth and saieth to doe it without pain, and (as it were) not minding it.[5]

Comfort of range equally encourages a facility of gesture and nuance that the physical demands of extreme register may preclude. However, two factors are important to acknowledge. One is that the extremes of range themselves may have important values that transposition subverts. Higher registers may infuse the music with an added sense of dramatic edge, and extended higher registers will tend toward greater clarity and greater carrying power.[6] Palestrina, for instance, reports to the Duke of Mantua in a letter of 1578 that he has used upward transposition to make things brighter.[7] And in the other direction, extended lower registers may, with darkness of timbre, underscore solemnity of affection and gravity of text.[8] So while naturalness may be the reigning default value, extended ranges may be intended for expressive affects of various sorts.

Often enough the attempt to move a work into a comfortable range for one part will disadvantage another, and decisions about which line to favor, which part to privilege, might well be made to enhance expressive goals. For example, much of the music of the famous Eton College Choirbook (ca. 1500) features an expanded range of often over four octaves; that is, the bass parts are low and the treble parts soar into a high tessitura. A sympathetic downward transposition may gain smiles from the treble section, but it will challenge the basses to render their lines clearly or with volume adequate to balance the treble. And the gain in naturalness in one part seems bought at the price of unnaturalness in another. Moreover, the lowered version also works against the sense of drama and flourish that seems much a part of these antiphons. And as they seem to proceed from a desire to create an unusual special sonic effect—many voices over an extended compass—the brilliant timbre of the unlowered treble has much to recommend it. Moreover, given the thickness that accrues to writing in so many parts, the brilliance of the high range is highly effective in carving out its own sonic space.

A similar situation may be found in the large-scale Magnificat and the psalm "Lauda Ierusalem" in Monteverdi's Vespers of 1610. There is considerable theoretical evidence[9] in support for these movements being performed a fourth below their notated pitch. And as is stunningly apparent in comparing alternate versions, the change of character is perhaps the biggest point of contrast. At the high pitch, the cornetts "dare" the heights in dramatic ascents; at the lower pitch drama gives way to richness of timbre. One version is an exercise in strength and control, the other an opportunity for sonic fullness. Thus, in these and other examples, although we may approach the repertory with a sense of free choice about pitch, we must also recognize that each decision of pitch level affects much more than just pitch; it radically changes balance, timbre, and character.

So, if there is an assumed looseness regarding notated pitch and its relationship to a fixed pitch standard, it does not mean that questions of pitch level are insignificant. As we have suggested above, expression, timbre, and constitution of the ensemble all may be strongly affected by a decision for one pitch level versus another. Moreover, several things, as David Fallows has observed, suggest that the absence of pitch standard was more characteristic of the earlier rather than the later Renaissance.[10] For example, the increased frequency of collaboration between choir and instruments suggests that, at least on those occasions, a pitch standard was secure. And in addition, the development of clef codes that indicate transposition seems to embody the notion that a specific pitch level was desired, albeit not the one notated. In other words, there would be no need to encode levels of transposition if one had full freedom to place the work wherever.

Contemporary sources describe a downward transposition for works appearing in the so-called *chiavette* (*chiavi alti* or high clef) configuration that appears in the sixteenth and early seventeenth centuries. In a four-voice texture, the high clef configuration is notated with the soprano part in treble clef, the alto with a c-clef on the second line (mezzo-soprano clef), the tenor with a c-clef on the third line (alto clef), and the bass with a c-clef on the fourth line or an f-clef on the third line (baritone clef). A transposition downward of a fourth or a fifth—as is encoded here—tends to bring these lines then into conformity with more standard s, a, t, b ranges, while the notation with the high clefs helps to avoid leger lines.[11] However, from a historical perspective, one needs to be alert to the dangers of circularity here; the idea of a "standard range" for any voice part might be suspect given the tradition of pitch flexibility described above. Moreover, attempts to base the "standard range" of historical voices—and thus also what would have been considered extreme—on the ranges of their modern counterparts is perilous. Indeed, different modes of training may well suggest differences in "natural range," as do documented historical changes in physiology. This has been well underscored in Simon Ravens's study of the countertenor in Tudor England.[12] Ravens draws on documentary studies correlating laryngeal size, bodily height, and vocal range, wherein height becomes a significant predictor of the size of the larynx and thus the vocal range. Focusing on Tudor England, he uses the evidence of such things as door frames and effigies, and is able to suggest that the Tudor English were normatively shorter than we are today. Moreover, with the emergence of specific data in the eighteenth century, he can show that in mid-eighteenth-century England the average adult height was 64.97 inches, as compared to 68.9 inches in 1984. Thus he reasonably speculates that "between 1550 and 1998 the average height of an English adult male has risen by between 5 and 7 inches." And from this he concludes that the average voice would thus have been higher.[13] In this light we must be careful not to project modern norms on historical voices.

One of the more visible manifestations of high-pitch singing does in fact relate to the Tudor and Jacobean repertories, here generally taking concrete evidence from the Jacobean context and speculatively applying it backward onto the earlier era.[14] Jacobean organs were transposing instruments, whereon depressing the "c" key gives the choir pitch "f", and as we can discern from surviving instruments, this choir "f" corresponded to a modern a-flat. This then is compelling documentation of the need in Jacobean music to transpose choral notation up a minor third. In addition, this expansion of the high register, which obviously changes the disposition of the ensemble, sees the labeling of trebles as both "treble" and "mean" to account for the additional treble parts. As this pertains to Thomas Tomkins, might it also pertain to

Thomas Tallis? Is it reasonable to project this backward a generation or two? Several have taken up this cause. Roger Bray, for instance, cites both the similar dimensions of a surviving Tudor organ and extant Jacobean organ cases, and also the indications in the early sixteenth-century Caius Choirbook where pieces beginning on "F" have annotations like "ut in c fa ut" or "c fa ut"—here seeming to indicate that the organist play the "c" key in order to give the "f" to the singer. If the Tudor organ is then a transposing instrument like the Jacobean, perhaps the choral pitch standard is also similar.[15]

MUSICA FICTA

Flexible pitch standards and transposition codes are examples of the ways in which early notation was often an example of "what you see is not necessarily what you get." Perhaps one of the most pervasive examples of this is the performer-added, accidental inflections of *musica ficta*. The scale of the gamut, the body of notes theoretically existing, was known as *musica recta* (see ex. 4.1). Significantly, though all notes were *singable*, not all the notes that were sung were part of the gamut, that is, part of the theoretically constructed scale. For purposes of avoiding dissonances and awkward contours, as well as for enhancing the gravitational pulls of voice leading, theorists advised that performers inflect the notes of *musica recta* by half steps, often altering them to notes from outside the system—the "false" notes of *musica ficta*.[16] Thus, for instance, the common alteration of a "c" to c-sharp at a "d" cadence, enhancing the voice leading, replaces a note within the gamut with one from without. Half-step inflections, however, are available within *musica recta* at the pitch "b," as seen above. Because this half-step inflection is *musica recta*, not *musica ficta*, it takes priority over other alterations that may suggest themselves in a given context. A simultaneous or consecutive f-b would typically require inflection to render the interval perfect. While either an f-sharp or a b-flat would suffice, the b-flat becomes the sanctioned choice because it is *musica recta* whereas the f-sharp is not. Similarly, vertical issues take priority over linear ones, as asserted by Tinctoris and Giovanni del Lago.[17] The choice of inflections was codified, but not monolithic, a factor that, along with the fact that *musica ficta* was being added by the performers themselves, introduces the notion of variability in the actual pitch content of any given, sung work.

e″	e la
d″	d la sol
c″	c sol fa
b-nat.	b mi
b-flat	b fa
a′	a la mi re
g′	g sol re ut
f′	f fa ut
e′	e la mi
d′	d la sol re
c′	c sol fa ut
b-nat.	b mi
b-flat	b fa
a	a la mi re
g	g sol re ut
f	f fa ut
e	e la mi
d	d sol re
c	c fa ut
B	b mi
A	a re
G	g ut [gamma ut][18]

Example 4.1 *Musica Recta*—the Notes of the Gamut

Theorists grouped the alterations under headings of "necessity" (*causa necessitatis*) and "beauty" (*causa pulchritudinis*).[19] Items of necessity include the prohibition of singing mi against fa, that is, no simultaneous or linear tritones (e.g., f fa ut against b mi), nor any simultaneous false relations (e.g., b-mi against b fa); and also the use of a half step above the syllable la, immortalized in the rhyme "una nota super la, semper est canendum fa" (a note above la is always sung as fa). This not only provides a downward gravitational pull that "caps" the top of a hexachord, but it avoids tritones that might arise in melodic context (see ex. 4.2).[20]

Example 4.2.

Under the heading of "beauty" are alterations that provide leading tones, major thirds at final (and some internal) cadences, imita-
tions retaining the same solmisations (and thus the same half-step
configurations), and cadential formations that find perfect consonances approached by the nearest imperfect consonance. In other
words, at a cadence one voice must approach by half step. Thus

  a. unisons are approached by minor, not major thirds
  b. fifths are approached by major, not minor thirds
  c. octaves are approached by major, not minor sixths

Much of the practice of *musica ficta* is syntactical, acknowledging
the gravitational pulls of half-step voice leading and the amenity of
perfected intervals. The effect of the employment of these principles
of good singing is to enhance the smoothness of the linear flow, the
logic of the resolutions, and the overall sweetness.[21] While many of
the alterations are obligatory, some are discretionary, and those that
are obligatory may not always have a clear-cut application. Thus the
application of *musica ficta* is to a degree interpretative, and where
choices emerge, the expressive implications of maximizing sweetness or not should prove influential.

INTONATION

The quality of sweetness furthered by *musica ficta* is, of course, also
profoundly indebted to pure systems of intonation, and herein lies
one of the most striking contrasts between modern and historic
style.[22] Modern choirs, despite the inherent flexibility to tune as they
wish, are overwhelmingly influenced by the equal temperament of
the modern piano. And again, while its tyranny is not unbreakable,
its bonds are strong. Prior to the general adoption of equal temperament in the late eighteenth and early nineteenth centuries, tuning
systems were founded on pure, beatless intervals; tuning systems
varied principally by the choice of which intervals were kept as pure
as possible. Pythagorean tuning was based on a pure beatless fifth,
complementing the primary status of that interval (and its inversion
the fourth) in medieval counterpoint. Thirds in this system were im-
pure, and this was echoed by their contemporary status as dissonant
intervals, and thus their instability in counterpoint. The dramatic

change in music in the early fifteenth century—the stunningly sweet sonorities of English discant, for example—catapult the third to new prominence both linearly and vertically. This is accompanied then by changes in tuning to systems based on the pure third, such as meantone tuning. Just intonation is a system wherein fifths and thirds both are beatless and pure.[23]

Thus, one of the primary obstacles the modern singer faces in dealing with earlier repertories is adopting a style of production that will allow intervals to be heard as beatless and learning to sing thirds narrow enough to achieve their beatless purity.[24] Efforts extended toward this goal are infinitely worthwhile. The frequency of pure intervals clarifies the sound in ways that well serve both the general timbre and the contrapuntal structure of much Renaissance music. Moreover, in unequal temperament, harmonic tension is intensified and cadential resolution both sweetened and given a greater sense of repose and stability.

Cultivating the ability to sing the requisite pure thirds of Renaissance polyphony will likely necessitate a time of reorientation, although once the sound and placement of the narrow thirds become familiar, an almost somatic memory may take over and require little prompting thereafter. It can be fruitful to vary the way one describes the narrow thirds. While often it is expeditious to say simply, "sing the upper note lower," that can lead to an overcompensation that makes things flat and the sound and tuning tense (certainly the opposite of its intended affect). Verbal instructions that ask for a more "relaxed" third, a "sweeter" third, or a "more stable" third may bring you to the desired pitch more quickly. In addition, the clarity of the pure intervals themselves offers a quality that singers may find a more immediately achievable goal than abstractions of tuning. That is, the pure interval "rings" with a clarity that is somatically memorable, and aiming for that "ring" may produce the desired intonation more quickly and easily than a direct assault on the tuning itself.

Much of the choral singer's sense of intonation is nurtured by placing his or her part in relation to another part. Even though we might easily construct and practice a meantone scale, say, its pitches are determined by vertical relationships. The modern practice of singing from score allows one—perhaps tempts one—to sing with an *eye* open to these relationships. That is, seeing that one's note is the third of a triad will prompt one to adjust accordingly. However,

Renaissance singing from score was exceedingly rare. Thus it is inescapable that one sang one's lines with the *ear* strongly alert to the harmonic contexts and affinities—quite a different thing from seeing them and intellectually processing the ramifications. In turn, this aurally harmonic sense of the individual line also nurtures the expression of the line itself, investing it with more layers to guide its emphases and shaping of contours.

NOTES

1. In Carol MacClintock, *Readings in the History of Music in Performance* (Bloomington: Indiana University Press, 1979), 62. See also Bernhard Ulrich, *Concerning the Principles of Voice Training during the A Cappella Period and until the Beginning of Opera (1474–1640),* trans. John W. Seale (Minneapolis, Minn.: Pro Musica Press, 1973), 77.

2. In Ulrich, *Principles,* 77–78.

3. See "On Singing and the Vocal Ensemble II," in *A Performer's Guide to Renaissance Music,* ed. Jeffery T. Kite-Powell (New York: Schirmer, 1994), 33.

4. See "Chant," in *A Performer's Guide to Medieval Music,* ed. Ross W. Duffin (Bloomington: Indiana University Press, 2000), 14. Roger Bowers also forges a relationship between chant range and that of polyphony in "The Performing Pitch of English 15th-c. Church Polyphony," *Early Music* 8 (1980): 21–28.

5. Trans. Sir Thomas Hoby, 1561 (London: J. M. Dent, 1956), 45–46.

6. Recently, while seated in the nave of a large gothic-styled cathedral, I listened to a well-trained choir of men and boys sing a festival service from their traditional position, decani and cantoris behind the choir screen. While the men were easily heard, the audibility of the boys depended much on range. Above a certain point in the register, the sound had an easy presence; below that point, however, the sound, regardless of the volume that I suspect was actually being produced, tended to disappear. Cf. Barry Rose's remarks on singing in London's St. Paul's Cathedral: "I like high pitch because it suits the building in that key: the higher the key the more clearly it carries in St. Paul's." In Peter Phillips, "The Golden Age Regained 2," *Early Music* 8 (1980): 185.

7. "Piu allegra." See James Haar, "Value Judgements in Music of the Renaissance," in *Companion to Medieval and Renaissance Music* (New York: Schirmer, 1992), 20.

8. In commenting on Josquin's four-voice setting of De Profundis, Glareanus (1547) connects the motet's low range with the specific overtones of the text. See Kenneth Kreitner's well-reasoned study, "Very Low Ranges in the Sacred Music of Ockeghem and Tinctoris," *Early Music* 14 (1986): 472.

9. See Andrew Parrott's compendious study, "Transposition in Monteverdi's Vespers of 1610: An 'Aberration' Defended," *Early Music* 12 (1984): 490–516. For a recent, more conservative view, see Roger Bowers, "An 'Aberration' Reviewed: The Reconciliation of Inconsistent Clef-Systems in Monteverdi's Mass and Vespers of 1610," *Early Music* 31 (2003): 527–38.

10. David Fallows, "The Performing Ensembles in Josquin's Sacred Music," *Tijdschrift van de Vereniging voor Nederlandse Muziekgeschiedenis* 35, nos. 1/2 (1985): 47.

11. See Herb Myers, "Pitch and Transposition," in Kite-Powell, *A Performer's Guide,* 252, and Jeffrey Kurtzman, *The Monteverdi Vespers of 1610: Music, Context, Performance* (Oxford: Oxford University Press, 1999), 409.

12. Simon Ravens, "A Sweet Shrill Voice: The Countertenor and Vocal Scoring in Tudor England," *Early Music* 26 (1998): 123–34.

13. Ravens, "A Sweet Shrill Voice," 124

14. See David Wulstan, *Tudor Music* (London: Dent, 1985); J. Bunker Clark, *Transposition in Seventeenth Century English Organ Accompaniments and the Transposing Organ* (Detroit: Information Coordinators, 1974); and Roger Bray, "More Light on Early Tudor Pitch," *Early Music* 8 (1980): 35–42.

15. Bray, "More Light," 37. For a recent revision of the high-pitch theory, see Andrew Johnstone, "'As It Was in the Beginning': Organ and Choir Pitch in Early Anglican Church Music," *Early Music* 31 (2003): 507–25. Johnstone argues for a less extreme choir pitch of A = c. 475 Hz.

16. The idea of half-step "inflection" is convenient for our discussion, with its implication that one moves a pitch to a neighboring pitch that is adjacent by a chromatic step. However, this concept of inflection is an anachronism, as Rob Wegman has underscored, because it requires that the neighbor tone be there in the first place. And *musica recta*, the Gamut, did not have adjacent half steps throughout its range. See "Musica Ficta," in *Companion to Medieval and Renaissance Music*, 272. In our discussion the word "inflection" will be retained out of convenience.

17. See Karol Berger, "Musica Ficta" in *Performance Practice: Music before 1600,* ed. Howard Mayer Brown and Stanley Sadie (New York: W. W. Norton, 1990), 115.

18. From this lowest note we derive the name "Gamut" for the entire range of pitches in *musica recta*, and from there, more generally, to refer to the full scope of something.

19. Modern discussions of *musica ficta* are plentiful. See, for example, Karol Berger, *Musica Ficta: Theories of Accidental Inflections in Vocal Polyphony.* . . . (Cambridge: Cambridge University Press, 1987); Rob Wegman, "Musica Ficta," in the *Companion to Medieval and Renaissance Music*, 265–74; and Berger, *Musica Ficta*. Particularly congenial is Nicholas Routley's "A Practical Guide to *musica ficta,"* *Early Music* 13 (1985): 59–71, which I follow here.

20. The Gamut was divided into hexachords beginning on G, C, and F. By the technique of "mutation," a singer might move from the syllables

of one hexachord to another, allowing pitches to be renamed and recontextualized.

21. Cf. Prosdocimo de' Beldomandi (1412), who asserts regarding the alteration of cadential intervals that "there is no other reason for this than a sweeter-sounding harmony. Why the sweeter-sounding harmony results from this can be ascribed to the sufficiently persuasive reason that the property of the imperfect thing is to seek the perfect, which it cannot do except through approximating itself to the perfect. This is because the closer the imperfect consonance approaches the perfect one it intends to reach, the more perfect it becomes, and the sweeter the resulting harmony." *Contrapunctus,* trans. Jan Herlinger (Lincoln: University of Nebraska Press, 1984), 83–85.

22. For discussion, see Ross Duffin, "Tuning and Temperament," in Kite-Powell, *A Performer's Guide,* 238–47.

23. While the third gained prominence and theoretical consonance in the fifteenth century, its inherent stability would only gradually emerge, as witnessed in the tendency of composers like Ockeghem and Josquin to include the third in a final cadence, but withdraw it before the chord has reached completion.

24. How narrow is a meantone third? Quantified in cents (100 cents represent a half step in equal temperament), the following gives comparative values for the major third in different temperaments: Pythagorean = 408 cts.; equal = 400 cts.; quarter-comma meantone = 386 cts.

Chapter 5

Rhythm, Tempo, and the Conductor's Gesture

When Renaissance theorists likened the slow, governing beat of the tactus to the human heartbeat, they engaged a model that would not only help determine speed but would, at least metaphorically, also confirm that the basic rhythmic pulse of a work is a central concern, a matter of the "heart" of the piece. This central concern embracing questions of tempo, proportion, and accent may be easily misunderstood, especially in the gap between modern and historical approaches.

Renaissance concepts of the way in which temporal space is organized seem closely akin to the hierarchical harmony of physical space that one finds in gothic cathedrals. The vast verticality of the space, drawing the eye heavenward, presents a number of horizontal strata—layers that each have their own spatial integrity, layers in which the eye may gratifyingly linger, layers that have their own organizational syntax. But perhaps the most striking element is not perceived in the individual layers of pier arcade, triforium, and clerestory; the most striking element seems to be the rhythmic harmony of the layers one with another, born of an easily perceived proportional relationship. Looking vertically at Salisbury Cathedral, for instance (see figure 5.1), the pier arcade, the largest of the units, contains a two-window subdivision within its fundamental arch; above it, the smaller triforium contains a four-part subdivision; above it, the medial size of the clerestory is subdivided into three. Translated into rhythmic terms, it is on bottom a whole-note layer with subdivided half notes, above which is a half-note layer with subdivided quarter notes, and above them all a layer of half-note triplets. Each layer is convincing in its own right, but the harmony of the layers seems paramount. And for that harmony to emerge, the largest element, the arch of the pier arcade, *must be seen as a unit*, no less than the smaller ones. In musical terms, then, the *slowest* element must still assert a linear integrity, even the *fundamental* integrity, organizing the space of all the others. Yet we often encounter interpretations that are based on and organized by the faster levels to which the ear is easily drawn. Often we mistakenly organize around the rhythmic triforium or the clerestory, instead of the pier arcade, resulting in performances that have too many principal beats, and performances that, in not sensing the integrity of the arcade level, have in essence reduced the number of lines in the harmony of layers.

The starting place is the slow level, not the fast, and that level is the tactus, generally defined as the pulse dictated by the slow up and down motion of the hand. As Giovanni Maria Lanfranco wrote in 1533, the beat "is a particular sign formed in imitation of the pulse of a healthy person by means of a raising and a lowering of the hand of the person who conducts."[1] And in the white mensural notation of the sixteenth century, the tactus generally moved at the level of the semibreve, unless diminution was indicated to shift the tactus to the breve level. The idea of the slow tactus ruling the rhythm persisted past the time of white mensural notation, however. Schütz, for example, in the preface to his Easter oratorio, *Historia . . . der Aufferstehung . . . Jesu Christi* (1623), writes that the slow beat "represents the soul and life of all music."[2] By no means an indication that Schütz's music is to be sung slowly, it rather acknowledges that the slow level must move quickly enough to have its own perceptible rhythmic life. In example 5.1 from Schütz's Easter Oratorio, we see a fast-moving treble line, and we might be tempted to base our tempo on a speed that allows one to render it comfortably. However, if that accommodation is "too slow," it may rob the bass line of its rhythmic life. Following Schütz's lead, one might more fruitfully start with the heart and soul, the slower line, and fit the faster line into it.[3] In seventeenth-century music, that slower line, of course, is often the bass. As Josef Mertin observes: "the thoroughbass offers significant suggestions for the clarification of the main tempo, of the tactus. The bass line by itself as well as the essential harmonic events prescribed by the figures offer a much clearer reading of the basic motion than the upper voices."[4] In this context and earlier ones as well, it is important to note that this idea is not just a

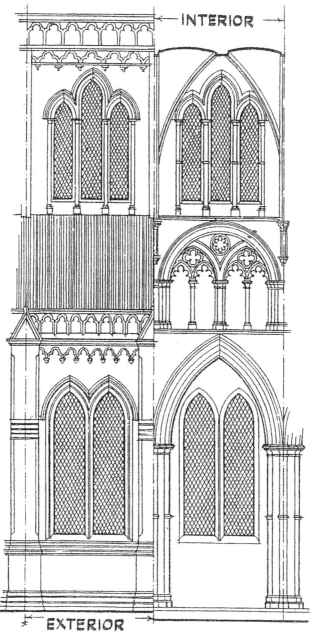

Figure 5.1. Salisbury Cathedral, from Martin S. Biggs, *Cathedral Architecture* (London: Pitkin Pictorials, 1979).

question of tempo—are you going fast enough so that the slow line
has integrity?—but a question of concept—are you conceiving the
slow line as important in its own right and as a unit that "contains"
the others? It is possible to go fast enough, and still miss the concept.

Example 5.1. Heinrich Schütz, *Historia der Aufferstehung,* 1623

So, the tactus is the basic unit whose integrity helps determine
speed. Its regular bounds, its temporal grid, also provides the framework for contrapuntal harmony. Cadential resolution, placement of
suspensions, placement of nonharmonic tones, etc., tend to be strictly
guided by their relation to the tactus. However, as much as the tactus
may assert itself in these ways—tempo and harmony—it had little if
anything to do with accent. The grouping of twos and threes were

myriad, often engagingly irregular and generally determined by context. And much of the interest in a line is animated by the tension between the regularity of the tactus and the melody's accentual freedom from it. A succession of even-numbered notes will naturally suggest duple accent schemes; uneven groupings may suggest triple schemes, as will ratios of notes. For example, a line in duple measure that moves |minim semibreve minim| semibreve minim semibreve, etc., may likely be perceived to be moving in simple triplets (see ex. 5.2a), regardless of where the tactus falls, even though the tactus meter may suggest a syncopated pattern in duple measure (see ex. 5.2b):

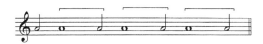

Example 5.2a.

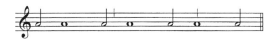

Example 5.2b.

Syncopation is not entirely ruled out, and in some contexts, like the following excerpt from the Eton Choirbook (see ex. 5.3), seems well aimed, adding a rhythmic vigor to a decidedly florid, decorated style.

Example 5.3.   Robert Wylkynson, "Salve Regina" (*Eton Choir Book*)

Melodic contour will often confirm the naturalness of the triple pattern; text underlay—admittedly often a variable item, only loosely indicated in the sources—can also reinforce the concept. Gioseffo Zarlino, in his *Le Istitutioni armoniche* (1558), acknowledges this relationship:

> adapt the words of the speech to the musical figures in such a way and with such rhythms that nothing barbarous is heard, not making short syllables long and long syllables short as is done every day in innumerable compositions, a truly shameful thing.[5]

The ease of seeing the patterns, too, is much enhanced by the absence of barlines (the visual image of the tactus). Barlines tempt us to consider syncopation; their absence, on the other hand, allows the triple patterns to emerge with ease.

In the end, the rhythmic groupings become part of an idiomatic syntax that, confirmed by context, is nevertheless nurtured by one's experience of idiom, especially one's somatic experience of it. Mertin writes that "every performing musician must develop his ability to experience rhythmic groupings, not by mechanical tricks, but by constant efforts to carry the manifold rhythms into consciousness."[6] And in experiencing these things, much of what one is experiencing is the natural tension between tactus and ametrically free melodic lines.

There are a number of sources that seek to give an objective measure of the tactus, and they do so often in somatic terms. For example, Franchinus Gaffurius (1496) likens the tactus to the unexcited human pulse.[7] In 1482 Bartolomeo Ramis de Pareia compared it to "an even moment between the diastole and systole of a body"; Lanfranco in 1533 noted that the tactus, as a raising and lowering of a leader's hand, imitates the motion of a healthy pulse; and Zarlino also suggested that the hand gesture for beating the tactus needed to "be regulated in its movement like the human pulse."[8] The frequency with which such comparisons occur *may* suggest to some the normative status of a tactus around MM 60, a beat per second. Provocatively, J. A. Bank has even proposed that the division of things into seconds may be naturally innate, citing the tendency of the pace of a natural walk to tend toward MM 60, as do the "principal percussions of speech patterns," regardless of language.[9] In other words, a tactus of MM 60 may be attuned to biological rhythms of various sorts, suggesting that the connection between the singer, the singing, and the singer's body is both natural and profound. Certainly the degree to which tactus is described in somatic terms (as above) and the degree to which tactus was enshrined in physical action—the steady up and down motion of the hand—invites us to understand the concept bodily. Our modern tendency to privilege the intellect over the body may thus challenge the very way in which we perceive the concept of tactus. Tactus is less something that is thought—an intellectual system of abstractions—as it is something that one knows in the body and through the body.[10] One challenge, certainly, to the modern conductor of early music is to understand tempos somatically and to develop ways of rehearsal that nurture that understanding in the singers under her direction. It may be as simple as having all the singers beat the slow-moving tactus as they sing; it may be as simple as stepping the slow-moving tactus as one sings; regardless, tactus is something that is physically understood, physically moved. The 1434 description by Georgius Anselmus of singers tapping the tactus on each other's hands or backs is a fetching image of how a group might come to understand the tempo physically, together. He writes:

> According to one school of thought, that mensura is sufficiently close to a medium [length of] time in which a singer, while neither quickening a piece too much nor prolonging [it] in long note[s], taps the toe of his foot, keeping his heel to the ground, or taps his hand against his disciple's hand or back as evenly as possible.[11]

However, whether the tendency to somatic description means a fixed tempo is quite another matter altogether. The proposition, simply put, is if descriptions of the tactus so recurrently refer to standard measures like the human pulse, may we assume that those standards are the *only* value for the tactus? The extensive aesthetic emphasis on proportion seems to offer a measure of support, because through it a considerable variety of tempo variation was possible, while still understanding the tactus as standard. That is to say, the proportional manipulation of the tactus can achieve a wide range of speeds, analogous to a range in which the beat is understood to be fully a matter of free choice. Moreover, in music before the seventeenth century, indications of tempo by anything other than proportional manipulation is exceedingly rare. One might interpret that extreme rarity as symptom of a casual attitude toward tempo: Nothing is indicated because you are free to choose what you will. However, it seems far more likely that the rarity—in reality, a near total absence—of tempo indications derives from a musical language that had such a conventionalized understanding of tempo that no indication was necessary.

Support for a view of tempo as fixed comes from wide-ranging sources. For example, Savanarola, around 1440, interestingly reversed the somatic equation. He suggested that medical doctors could have a measure of a healthy heart rate by consulting the musicians, normalizing a tempo that "could be learned from a good musician in eight hours."[12] We have gone to physiology for our musical understanding; Savanarola goes to music for physiological understanding. Had tempo been wide ranging, would he have done so?

In certain quarters at certain junctures the theoretical discussion of tempo does advocate fixed tempo—but this may be a long way from general application. Alexander Blachly, in his masterful dissertation, "Mensuration and Tempo in 15th-Century Music,"[13] notes for instance that constant tactus emerges most dogmatically in the writings of Sebald Heyden (*De Arte Canendi*, 1540). For example, Heyden writes that, "Many kinds of *tactus* cannot occur in a relation of proportions, but of necessity only one and the same kind of unchanging *tactus*." And further, "If some current arithmetician, in teaching computations, were to introduce many species of the unit one that were mutually different in quantity, and compared them to other numbers in proportions, what, I ask, would he have done but to obscure not only *ratio* and precept of the proportions, but also to create a relationship that was plainly insoluble?"[14]

If Heyden is clear, the applicability of his view is not, and there is much to suggest that the fixed tactus he advocates was not universal in the Renaissance. Among other things, one can presume that the complexity of a work, the size of the ensemble, the degree of preparation, and the acoustic environment would all influence the choice of speed, then, as now.[15] One might also expect affectivity or the degree of solemnity to be influential. In a late fifteenth-century chant treatise, Conrad von Zabern observed that the speed at which chant was sung was proportional to the solemnity of the feast. It does not seem a wild stretch to extend this idea to polyphony, as well.[16] Some did, in fact, such as Vicentino and Zarlino.[17] In *L'Antica musica* Vicentino notes, for example, "having matched the steps and leaps with the consonances and dissonances, a composer should then confer on them a rate of motion appropriate either to the subject inherent in the words or to other ideas. Such motion is commonly called air. Thus, if either a composition on certain words or one without a text proceeds at a seemly pace, some people will say, 'The work has a fine air'—but this is not proper usage."[18]

Others spoke unequivocally of tempo variability. Praetorius, in the early years of the seventeenth century, for example, roots tempo change in relation to the text:

> The tempo of a performance must not be hurried, or even the most delightful ensemble will sound confused. With a slower beat, however, the music is more agreeable and can be grasped better. . . . But to use, by turns, now a slower, now a faster beat, in accordance with the text, lends dignity and grace to a performance and makes it admirable.[19]

Blachly offers an extensive discussion of Tinctoris and tempo, and one of the most telling passages against strictly fixed tempo concerns Tinctoris's remark that in a certain work, the time signature O2/1 is impractical because a certain passage is too difficult at that speed.[20]

The implication, then, is that either the proportional equivalence is not literal (see below), that is, O2/1 is not literally twice as fast as O, or else the tactus for O may itself vary, in this case to the slower side to accommodate the difficult passage. Either way, the case of a flexible latitude in reading proportion or a flexible approach to the tactus, the notion of a strict, unvarying sense of "the" speed, is subverted and replaced with a degree of choice. However, the degree of choice need not, and likely was not, a broad one, embracing any speed one might choose. Rather a flexibility that maintains at least an approximate proportionality, tempered by affective and practical concerns, seems appropriate.

Blachly's conclusion is an elegant one that places the choice of tempo in the company of other expressive decisions—ultimately a matter of aesthetic choice rather than mathematical predeterminism: He writes, "the speed of the beat may be decided by the performer according to the perceived needs of each piece, and of each section of a larger piece. Tempo is thus removed from the domain of non-musical, mathematical criteria and restored to the domain of performance, where it keeps company with such notions as phrasing, tone color, mood, expression, declamation, gesture, and volume."[21]

Proportional notation—regardless of the degree to which it was strictly interpreted—was prevalent from the fifteenth on into the seventeenth century, and as the discussion above suggests, it was subject to latitude and varying interpretations. The strictest and most literal reading of the signs suggests that a slash will see the tactus note value double in speed. Note that this does not mean that the slow underlying pulse is doubled, but rather the note value through which that slow underlying pulse is conveyed. Thus where the unslashed signature finds the semibreve conveying the tactus, the slash will transfer that value and function to the breve. Reasonably, this will also enable faster notes to be conveyed in familiar, less complex notational values: The minim and the semiminim become rapid notes in the slashed time signature. Uneven proportional values, in the strictest and most literal reading of the signs, are read fractionally: O3/1 would be three semibreves moving in the time of one semibreve of O; O3/2 would be three semibreves moving in the time of two semibreves of O, and so forth. But the strict application did not always apply, as Blachly has shown for Tinctoris, and the passing of time would also see the meaning of the proportional signatures reinterpreted. For example, in the sixteenth century the shift from slashed C to slashed C3 implied the proportion of 2:3 at the level of the semibreve. However, in the seventeenth century, that same sign could imply the faster ratio of 1:3 at the level of the semibreve.[22] In the seventeenth century, the relationship of 3:2, the sesquialtera, which earlier could be indicated by a 3 alone, now would require the 3/2.[23] Banchieri, for instance, specifies that slashed C3/2 would find three semibreves moving in the time of two; C3/2 would also be a sesquialtera relationship now at the level of the minim; C3/1 would be a true tripla, with three semibreves moving in the space of one.[24] With Praetorius, in his landmark music encyclopedia, *Syntagma Musicum*, the C and slashed C retain distinctions, but the meaning is general and no longer proportional. He writes:

> Nowadays both signs [C and slashed C] are observed for the most part such that C is used mainly in madrigals and slashed C mainly in motets. Because madrigals and other pieces which abound with semiminims and fusae under the sign C proceed in faster motion, wheras motets, which abound with breves and semibreves under the sign slashed C, proceed in a slower motion, for that reason, the latter work

will be measured by a faster tactus, the former by a slower, which stands as a mean between two extremes, lest a too-slow motion lead to fatigue in the ears of the listeners, or a too-fast motion lead to a headlong fall, just as the horses of the sun ran off with Phaeton, who gave no heed to the reins of the chariot.

For this reason, it does not appear wrong to me that composers mark with the sign C motets and other sacred pieces when they abound with black notes, announcing thereby that the tactus must be slower and weightier.

Each person, however, can reflect on each case himself, and, out of consideration of the text and the setting, observe where a slower or where a faster tactus must be used.[25]

Praetorius, then, does not say that the signs are interchangeable or without specific meaning, but the meaning is general—faster, but how much faster is not clear—and his description places the decision of how fast a tactus will go in the context of familiarly modern performer discretion, influenced by text and setting.

Overall, then, the evidence for objective values for the tactus and unflaggingly strict interpretations of proportional relationships cannot claim universal applicability. This should not blind us, however, to the still strong aesthetic of proportion that holds sway in much of this repertory, regardless of how strictly it is pursued. And in the service of that aesthetic, tempo choices that give integrity to all levels of organized time, especially the slower levels where the tactus is rooted, have a high priority, for much of the temporal beauty proceeds from sensing the relation of the large to the small, the macrocosm to the microcosm. If the macrocosm is too large (too slow) to be perceived, its temporal harmony with the smaller (faster) level cannot be perceived.

The word "tactus," with its resonance of tactility and its identity as a somatic action as well as an intellectual abstraction, places it centrally in a discussion of the act of conducting itself. One early, long-lived, and mainstream understanding of the tactus is that it is that which is indicated by the up and down motion of the arm, an equal, even motion in duple meter—down on one, up on two—or an unequal motion in three—down on one and two, up on three. In the context of the more elaborate beat patterns that emerge in the eighteenth century[26] this up and down motion seems simple, especially given the degree of rhythmic complexity and ametrical rhythmic freedom that often characterizes Renaissance music.

Our knowledge of conducting before the Renaissance is sketchy. One might well assume that the interest in chironomy of various sorts (the Guidonian Hand, for example, or the speculated link between the shape of neumes and hand gestures that might indicate melodic contours) would make the manual leading of a group of singers a familiar task. Mertin makes fetching reference to the example of polyphonists at Notre Dame swaying together, presumably keeping time with the motion of their bodies.[27] Here the important principle is that the keeping of the time was somatic, and it was corporate. We see a latter-day remnant in a late fifteenth-century illumination from the "Gradual of King Corvinus."[28] Here a number of singers are gathered around a common lectern. Several figures gesture with their hands; the "director" seems singled out by using both of his hands for the gestures. He also faces the lectern, not the singers. From this again, we get the notion that keeping time is something one does, rather than something one watches. With the "director" here facing the lectern, his visibility to the other singers is limited, confined more to a sidelong, peripheral look, as compared to the modern paradigm of trying to see conductor and music all in the same field of vision. And the timekeeping is not restricted to a single individual—timekeeping is something one does together as a group. One may reasonably expect a variety of practice to have existed, and certainly with the passage of time, the modern model of a *single timekeeper to be watched* does emerge, but it is telling how beneficial sharing the somatic tactus remains.

Moving the tactus together has a remarkable effect on ensemble coordination, to be sure. But it has an especially salubrious effect on getting a group to feel the integrity of the slow-moving tactus and the rhythmic hierarchy it implies. In essence, instructing an ensemble to *think* in one-to-the bar units is one thing; telling them to *feel* the motion in one-to-the bar units is another, and generally more effective. Most effective of all, however, is having them embody that motion, be it with the traditional up-down hand gesture, the bodily sway, the clapping of hands, or the motion of feet. While one will hardly ever imagine performing in that fashion, to have rehearsed in that way leaves an indelibly powerful stamp on the rhythmic understanding of the music. And that understanding, once again, focuses on the integrity of the slow-moving underlying pulse. Moreover, I suspect that embodiment of this sort nurtures physical investment in other aspects of the singing, as well. Embodiment in one aspect feeds embodiment in others. If the singer has invested herself bodily in the understanding of the rhythm, the bodily engagement of tone, etc., will likely also be enhanced.

The embodied rhythm and its hierarchical inflection of foundational pulse can be fruitfully reinforced with exercises of "melodic reduction," as well. For example, if the number of melodic notes invites the singer to focus on the wrong rhythmic layer, singing a background version of the line may aid reorientation. For example, the beginning of J. S. Bach's well-known motet, "Der Geist hilft" (BWV 226), with its sixteenth-note rhythms, may lead to too many subdivisions of the basic one-to-a-bar pulse. However, reducing the line to its background level (see ex. 5.4), and singing this with embodied conviction, can often provide a helpfully new sense of the rhythmic hierarchy.

Example 5.4.   J. S. Bach, "Der Geist hilft," BWV 226

For all its virtues, shared physical timekeeping is not the reigning paradigm today, of course, and one must consider what the single individual as timekeeper is to do to provide temporal direction. Modern conductors trained in the metrical patterns of beat-keeping may find it difficult to relinquish these habitual gestures in favor of a simple beating of the tactus, but it is an important move. Actually, the phrase "simple beating of the tactus" may be misleadingly simplistic. It may suggest a mechanical and uninflected gesture—a gestural minimalism. But the up and down beating of the tactus can still encompass a variety of interpretative signals; it is just that its rhythmic content has been pruned of the extraneous. That extraneous material is nearly always problematic. I know of no single misinterpretation of early choral repertories more rampant than the introduction of too many beats. Conductors using conventional patterns, regardless of their own understanding of the rhythmic hierarchies or regardless of verbal instruction, will find it difficult to convey the primacy of the slower line. To say "feel it in one," while you move in a conventional four, is an unhelpful contradiction. Habit plays a part, of course. Conductors will keep to the patterns because, in part, they are deeply ingrained and they allow a close control of the events. (Significantly, close control seems a modern corollary to the shift from corporate timekeeper to timekeeper as an individual to be watched.) But the patterns also remain in our hands because of the difficulty of maintaining the simple tactus gesture at a relatively slow speed. Following the somatic analogies discussed above, one might find a tactus in the range of MM = 60 frequent, if not objectively normative. It is a speed at which control of a flowing, smooth gesture is possible, but also one that seems to invite a subdivision for the hand's sake. Accordingly, some conductors fall into the subdivided patterns to compensate for the difficulty of moving the slow time. Regrettably, this is a compensation that has the sad effect of introducing too many beats.

It is important to recognize that the modern patterns not only will often introduce too many beats but also will have little to do with the accentual flow of the melodic lines, lines that in sixteenth-century polyphony will frequently be animated by an ametric rhythmic freedom, described above. For that reason, too, the beating of the slower line is helpful. However, there are a number of instances where beating the rhythmic contour of the ametric line is helpful. For example, where there are strong senses of new downbeats within the metrical frame of the tactus, they can be naturally and effectively indicated by gesture.

NOTES

1. In Alexander Blachly, "Mensuration and Tempo in 15th-Century Music" (Ph.D. diss, Columbia University, 1995), 209.

2. George J. Buelow, "A Schütz Reader: Documents on Performance Practice," *American Choral Journal* 27, no. 4 (1985): 14.

3. Cf. Josef Mertin, *Early Music: Approaches to Performance Practice,* trans. Siegmund Levarie (Irig, 1978; reprint, New York: Da Capo Press, 1986), 26. "The era of Schütz, entirely within the framework of the great cappella tradition, still knows fast tempi only as subdivisors and apprehends them only in relation to the large overall order."

4. Mertin, *Early Music,* 31.

5. In Curt Sachs, *Rhythm and Tempo* (New York: W. W. Norton, 1953), 253.

6. Mertin, *Early Music,* 22.

7. See Howard Mayer Brown, in *Performance Practice: Music before 1600,* ed. Howard Mayer Brown and Stanley Sadie (New York: W. W. Norton, 1990), 155.

8. In Jeffrey Kurtzman, *The Monteverdi Vespers of 1610: Music, Context, Performance* (Oxford: Oxford University Press, 1999), 435–36. That the somatic descriptors may only be analogies rather than literal prescriptions is suggested by Dale Bonge, "Gaffurius on Pulse and Tempo: A Reinterpretation," *Musica Disciplina* 36 (1982): 167–74.

9. J. A. Bank, *Tactus, Tempo, and Notation in Mensural Music from the 13th to the 17th Century* (Amsterdam: Annie Bank, 1972), 9–11.

10. A conductor seeking to recall a tempo may call to mind a mental "playback" of the music at a particular speed—common enough, one suspects—but another approach, and one close to the ideal here, would be to be guided by the muscle memory of the arms' motion at that particular speed.

11. In Blachly, "Mensuration and Tempo," 213.

12. Ephraim Segerman, "A Re-examination of the Evidence on Absolute Tempo before 1700," *Early Music* 24 (1996): 228.

13. (Ph.D. diss., Columbia University, 1995).

14. In Blachly, "Mensuration and Tempo," 302.

15. Cf. Alejandro Planchart, "Tempo and Proportions," in Brown and Sadie, *Performance Practice,* 126.

16. Joseph Dyer, "Singing with Proper Refinement: From *De Modo bene cantandi* by Conrad von Zabern (1474)," *Early Music* 6 (1978): 211.

17. Quoted in Kurtzman, *Monteverdi Vespers,* 454, n. 83.

18. Nicola Vicentino, *Ancient Music Adapted to Modern Practice,* trans. Maria Rika Maniates (New Haven, Conn.: Yale University Press, 1996), 86.

19. In Kurtzman, *Monteverdi Vespers,* 454.

20. Blachly, "Mensuration and Tempo," 183. Further, in a summary of Tinctoris's views on tempo, he suggests: "the attempt to double the speed of a voice written in O would result in 'a difficulty of performance or rather the destruction of all melody . . . because of the excessive speed,'" 196.

21. Blachly, "Mensuration and Tempo," 335.

22. Alejandro Planchart, "On Singing and the Vocal Ensemble II," in *A Performer's Guide to Renaissance Music,* ed. Jeffery T. Kite-Powell (New York: Schirmer, 1994), 35.

23. Planchart in Brown and Sadie, *Performance Practice,* 140.

24. In Kurtzman, *Monteverdi Vespers,* 447.

25. In Blachly, "Mensuration and Tempo," 449.

26. Mertin, *Early Music,* 35

27. Mertin, *Early Music,* 35.

28. Budapest, Nat. Szechenyi library Ms lat 424, fol. 41, reproduced in *Imago Musicae* 1 (1984): 81, fig. 3.

Chapter 6

Articulation, Ornamentation, and Interpretation

The articulation of early vocal music presents challenges to the modern singer, steeped in a technique that features depressed larynx, large air column, and a general slurring of notes for the sake of maximum uniformity and volume of tone. In particular, the challenges take the form of the need for increased verbalism and glottal articulation. Giovanni Camillo Maffei, an Italian physician and musician, notes in 1562 that rapid passage work was articulated in the throat, when he defines *voce passagiata* as "a sound caused by minute and ordered repercussions of air in the throat with the intention of pleasing the ear."[1] Similarly, Lodovico Zacconi, in his *Prattica di musica* (1596), observes:

> Two things are required for him who wishes to enter this profession [of singing]: chest and throat; chest, in order to be able to carry such a large number of notes [i.e., florid passage work] to a correct end; throat, to produce them easily. . . . [Some] because of defects of the throat, cannot separate the notes vigorously; that is, they cannot enunciate the notes well enough for it to be recognized as *gorgia*.[2]

This is echoed by Richard Wistreich's modern remarks on early "disposition":

> The ability to control rapid opening and closing of the glottis to make very fast and precise note articulation goes against normal modern vocal technique, dependent as the latter is on depressing the larynx. Nevertheless, the sources are absolutely clear on the matter, and without a flexible, swift and accurate disposition, no singer in the Renaissance,

Baroque, or Classical periods could hope to be taken seriously as a professional.[3]

Sally Sanford offers a similar view with regard to early Baroque singing:

> Both French and Italian singing in the seventeenth century differ significantly from modern singing with respect to the use of throat articulation, a technique for singing rapid passages and ornaments. Throat articulation had existed at least since the middle ages and had reached a zenith in the 1580's with *garganta* singers such as the three ladies of Ferrara, who excelled in this gorgia technique.[4]

The incompatibility with modern technique to which Wistreich refers is also underscored by Sanford, who extends the issue to an incompatibility with modern, pitch-fluctuation vibrato: "[T]he method to produce pitch fluctuation vibrato is in direct conflict with the mechanism to produce throat articulation. They cannot be used simultaneously."[5]

The early method of articulation rendered with glottal strokes produces a fluidity and clarity of sound that, aided by forward placement of the tone, is rich in its textural variety and strong in its capacity to heighten rhythm and melodic contours. Much insight can be gained by considering the articulative practice of early instruments. On all instruments, be they string, wind, or keyboard, the equivalent of the ultrasmooth modern slur was rare. Rather, all notes were normatively articulated, and at faster levels—levels that corresponded to the subdivisions of the tactus—articulations of successive notes were varied rather than repetitively equal. Thus, in example 6.1 a wind player would play passage work with a succession of syllables like *te re le re, te re le re* or *ti ri ti ri, ti ri ti ri*; a string player would render the same passage with separate bow strokes; a keyboard player would perhaps play it with 3, 4, 3, 4, (ascending) 3, 2, 3, 2 (descending).

te   re   le   re   te   re   le   re   te   3   4   3   4   3   2   3   2   3

Example 6.1.

Implicit in these articulations is a verbal, speechlike inequality, here paired as strong and weak successive notes. Significantly, too, even though the articulations group into pairs—small cells—*within* the cell there is a smooth fluidity. They are articulate at the level of a separate speech syllable, but generally flowing in the succession of syllables, as in the model of polysyllabic words. Thus the singer, by analogy, will want to avoid in melismas a peckiness that is too often the result of first attempts at glottal articulation; the articulateness need not, nor should not, be bought at the price of fluidity. Conrad von Zabern warns against this in his urging singers to avoid placing "h's" in front of melismatic syllables, a practice he criticizes as rustic.[6] Thus, in example 6.2 the singer might sing:

Example 6.2.

Exploring the analogy with instrumental articulation even more, we find that with certain instruments articulation is the sole means of creating accents, and this very much informs certain conventionalized phrasings. On instruments like the harpsichord or the organ, pressure of attack offers no means of conveying accent. Accordingly, players of those instruments habitually form accent with silence before the accented note. This conventional silence of articulation transfers effectively to the voice as well. In example 6.3, for instance, a cadential cliché features an ametrical freedom that positions a metrical offbeat as a strong note. Introducing space before it allows the accent to emerge without undue attention. This is effective before the note of resolution, as well.

Example 6.3.

The articulative silence will similarly invest pickup notes with an effectively anticipatory sense, as well as enhance the accent on the note that follows.

Moreover, the articulative silence is an effective means for achieving the grouping of figures. In example 6.4, ametrical triplets emerge in the line. To clarify the triplet grouping, shortening the third note not only marks the group off with silence but also heightens the accent of the first note of the triplet as well.

Example 6.4.

Contexts will naturally vary, and with them the length of the shortened note. However, in general it is wise to be aware that too short a note creates a false accent on the shortened note itself, and defeats the purpose of the articulative silence.

These principles of articulation—rarity of slur, articulation with the glottis, silence for grouping and accent—become with practice the natural adjuncts of the musical language. Much as we distinguish foreign languages not only by word content and structure, but also by the way in which things are pronounced, so too is articulation an integral part of the language of these earlier repertories.

Other gestures seem also to be a part of the musical language itself—conventionalized manners of rendering recurrent figures. The shaping of long notes into blossom and decay is a good example. In solo singing around 1600, this became enshrined in the ornament of the messa di voce. Like a balletic plié, a sinking in on a long note and rising from it dynamically (<>), it is described by Caccini in his *Le nuove musiche* as an exclamation "of increasing and abating of the voice."[7] Its expressive quality made it a popular gesture among instrumentalists as well.[8]

Distinctions between solo and choral singing are important to acknowledge, and there may well be an array of gestures in the soloist's quiver that do not translate well to group rendition. But given the frequency with which "choral" ensembles were one-to-a-part, and that choral establishments by no means closed the door to solo singers, ornaments like the messa di voce may well grace Baroque choral repertory.

The idea of shaped long notes is also nicely given form in the writings of the seventeenth-century English amateur, Roger North. In his *Notes of Me*, North draws diagrams of "plaine," "waived," and "trilled" notes, and graphically, the diagrams make clear that the notes are shaped and contoured. His verbal description is engaging as well. Regarding "pratique," after learning to sustain a "long, true, steddy and strong sound":

> I would have them learne to fill, and soften a sound, as shades in needlework, insensatim, so as to be like also a gust of wind, which bigins with a soft air, and fills by degrees to a strength, as makes all bend, and then softens away againe into a temper, and so vanish. And after this to superinduce a gentle and slow wavering, not into a trill, upon the swelling the note. Such as trumpetts use, as if the instrument were a litle shaken with the wind of its owne sound, but not so as to vary the tone, which must be religiously held to its place, like a pillar on its base, without the least loss of the accord.[9]

The messa di voce as a well-defined ornament emerges in the early seventeenth century. However, the idea of contoured, well-shaped long notes seems much at home in sixteenth-century polyphony as well, though justification is not explicit. By analogy, one might appeal to the roundness of poetic language and cadence or the rounded shapes in architecture and the visual arts—roundnesses that imbue things with a natural grace. One might also note that shaping notes becomes highly significant in straight-toned singing, for the shaping of notes, the molding of contours, keeps the straight tone from having a flat lifelessness or a machinelike quality. Andrea von Ramm has addressed this issue with reference to the "directing" of the note, a directing that I think is often the fruit of shape and contour. She writes:

> Singing should be pleasant for the listener as well as for the singer. Vibrato-less singing can be beautiful and pleasant, but that is only achieved when each note has a direction, the direction towards the next note. That is not necessarily a crescendo. It is rather an increase of tension right up to the cadence almost overlapping the next cadence. Vibrato-less singing succeeds only by guiding a musical line by breath control.[10]

Therefore, given the prominence of straight-tone singing in the sixteenth century, it seems safe to assume that shaping of long notes was an important complement to this tonal straightness. Moreover, one might also suggest that contour of the long note may provide a model for the phrase as a whole, that is, that the motion of the phrase is impelled toward a growth that will ebb in resolution.

In the seventeenth century, the messa di voce would have been part of an ornamental vocabulary, in this case a dynamic ornament. The subject of ornamentation has not typically been a pressing concern for choirs, generally because its improvisational basis seems awkward to implement by a group, and to "fix" the ornamentation so that a group might render it together is to make of it something altogether different. Nevertheless, repertories that we have long associated with choirs—like sixteenth-century polyphony—have often, if not normatively, been performed by a group of soloists, soloists who might well grace their lines with ornamental passage work. Thus, even though it will have little modern choral application, a basic knowledge of ornamental practice informs our understanding of a number of "choral" genres. Moreover, where solo ensembles are used or where instrumental doubling is employed, the ornamental practice described below may, in certain contexts, prove fruitful for singer and instrumentalist alike.

Ornamentation in the Renaissance, as Howard Mayer Brown long ago codified,[11] falls into two categories: stereotyped figures or graces, on the one hand, and divisions or diminutions, florid passage work, on the other. The stereotyped figures include various variations on pitch alternations, that is, trills and tremolos. Divisions or diminutions were made by dividing the space of slow, structural intervals into fast-moving, scalar passages, as illustrated in example 6.5.

Example 6.5. Diminutions from Giovanni Bassano, *Ricercate/Passaggi et Cadentie* (1585)

In forming the diminutions, most examples adhere to a pattern in which the background interval is the boundary of the division itself—the first and last note; the first note is returned to in the middle of the division as a way of keeping the original interval present in the ornamented version; and the background interval usually forms the conclusion of the division; that is, the last two notes of the division are the notes of the interval being divided (a pattern that ensures that awkward parallelisms can be avoided, etc.).[12] Grace and diminution were often combined in standard cadential formulas that feature both passage work and trill figures, as in example 6.6.[13]

Example 6.6. Cadences from Giovanni Bassano, *Ricercate/Passaggi et Cadentie* (1585)

To illustrate how this might be applied, we begin with the following excerpt from a Palestrina motet (see ex. 6.7).

Example 6.7. Giovanni da Palestrina, "Sicut cervus," part 2 (treble voice)

As the ornamentation is applied to the background level, not the foreground, we might next reduce the line to its basic structural intervals, as in example 6.8.

Example 6.8. Palestrina, "Sicut cervus," reduction to background (treble voice)

Some of these intervals may be chosen for diminution. Others may stay unaltered, in part to give a sense of the original melody. Still in other places, elements of the figural foreground may also be interestingly retained to good effect as part of the ornamental texture. Moreover, the cadence figure may be ornamented with figuration that combines both diminution and trill. Example 6.9 gives one possible ornamented version.

Example 6.9.   Palestrina, "Sicut cervus," with diminutions (treble voice)

Rendered with rapid velocity and glottal articulation, the passage becomes newly impressive . . . and soloistic. Does it have a relevance for *choral* performance of this literature? It is unlikely that embellishment by the choir was ever seen as practical or desirable. In discussing diminutions, Zacconi, for instance, clearly makes the distinction between choral and solo renditions of ensemble music: "Each time a singer wishes to find out if he is succeeding in his diminutions, he first will try them in company with other singers, *and those who have no companions on their parts* [emphasis added] can try it when all the voices form a full harmony."[14] However, on occasion it may be worthwhile experimenting with one singer introducing diminutions while the rest of the section remains on the written line. But regardless of whether the diminutions are present, they serve to remind the performer of the degree to which Renaissance singing aspired to be, among other things, *impressive.*[15]

One of the goals of interpretation is precisely to make such qualities palpable and present in the performance. The quality of impressiveness may derive from ornamentation, but equally so from a sense of scale, scoring, expressive gesture, and dynamic range.

While the qualities to be served are as varied as the performers, one guide to period qualities would be the strong sense of various affections and their musical corollaries. The idea of modes having affective particularity is, of course, an antique one, as is the idea that music prompts varied affective responses in the hearer. For example, Aristotle (following Plato) writes:

> [M]ele . . . do actually contain in themselves imitations of ethoses; and this is manifest, for even in the nature of the harmonia there are differences, so that people when hearing them are affected differently and have not the same feelings in regard to each of them, but listen to some in a more mournful and restrained state, for instance the so-called Mixolydian, and to others in a softer state of mind, for instance the relaxed harmoniai, but in a midway state and with the greatest composure to another, as the Dorian alone of the harmoniai seems to act, while the Phrygian makes men divinely suffused.[16]

And on the idea of affective response, Athenaeus records in the *Sophists at Dinner* that

> The Pythagorean Cleinias, for example, as Chamaeleon of Pontus records, whose conduct and character were exemplary, would always take his lyre and play on it whenever it happened that he was exasperated to the point of anger. And in answer to those who inquired the reason he would say, "I am calming myself down." So, too, the Homeric Achilles calmed himself with his kithara . . . which had the power of allaying his fiery nature.[17]

Sextus Empiricus, in recollecting those things that can be said on behalf of music (before he attempted to refute them), notes:

> Pythagoras, when he once observed how lads who had been filled with Bacchic frenzy by alcoholic drink differed not at all from madmen, exhorted the aulete who was joining them in the carousal to play his aulos for them in the spondeic melos. When he thus did what was ordered, they suddenly changed and were given discretion as if they had been sober even at the beginning.
> The Spartans, leaders of Hellas and famous for their manly spirit, would always do battle with music commanding them. And those who were subject to the exhortations of Solon drew up in battle order to the aulos and lyre, making the martial movement rhythmic.
> Just as music gives discretion to those who are frantic and turns the more cowardly toward a manly spirit, so also it soothes those who are inflamed by anger.[18]

The humanist backdrop to the Renaissance and the early Baroque era would keep this idea of affective response and affective particularity alive and well in the sixteenth and seventeenth centuries. Zarlino, for instance, in his *Le Istitutioni harmoniche*, part IV, details the emotional associations of the individual modes:

Mode 1—"has a certain effect midway between sad and cheerful"; "We can best use it with words that are full of gravity and that deal with lofty and edifying things."

Mode 2—Some have called it "a lamentful, humble and deprecating mode." "They have said that it was a mode fit for words which represent weeping, sadness, loneliness, captivity, calamity, and every kind of misery."

Mode 3—"Some have been of the opinion that the third mode moves one to weeping. Hence they have accommodated to it words which are tearful and full of laments."

Mode 4—"This mode is said . . . to be marvelously suited to lamentful words or subjects that contain sadness or supplicant lamentation, such as matters of love and to words which express languor, quiet, tranquillity, adulation, deception and slander."

Mode 5—"Some claim that, in singing, this mode brings to the spirit modesty, happiness, and relief from annoying cares. Yet the ancients used it with words or subjects that dealt with victory, and because of this some called it a joyous, modest, and pleasing mode."

Mode 6—Ecclesiastics "called it a devout and tearful mode, to distinguish it from the second mode, which is more funereal and calamitous."

Mode 7—"The words which are appropriate to this mode are said to be those which are lascivious or which deal with lasciviousness, those which are cheerful and spoken with modesty, and those which express threat, perturbation, and anger."

Mode 8—"Practicing musicians say that the eighth mode contains a certain natural softness and an abundant sweetness which fills the spirits of the listeners with joy combined with great gaiety and sweetness."

Mode 9—"[I]t possesses a pleasant severity, mixed with a certain cheerfulness and sweet softness."

Mode 10—"We may say that the nature of the tenth mode is not very different from that of the second and fourth modes."

Mode 11—"The eleventh mode is by its nature very suitable for dances. . . . Hence it has happened that some have called it a lascivious mode."

Mode 12—"[E]very composer who wishes to write a composition that is cheerful does not depart from this mode" [In psalmody] "it is a lamentful mode."[19]

Accordingly then, modern interpretations may be guided by these historical associations. Heightening the affective quality by musical means is no monolithic, objective matter. Sweetness may be reflected in softer dynamics; liveliness may suggest a faster tempo and perhaps a crispness of articulation, although keeping the traditional tactus tempo but adding fast, ornamental lines would also convey the same sense; melancholy and lament might be reflected in fewer numbers of singers, lower pitch levels, spareness of ornament, and extreme contouring of long notes; devotion and seriousness might likely slow the tempo. Thus once again, interpretation remains rich in performance choice.

The text is naturally a guide to the affective content, giving it a particularity that musical means alone cannot. In Zarlino's descriptions above, it is telling how often he refers to the connection between the mode and the words. Zarlino's concerns with the musical textual relationship go beyond this matter of affective association, however; he was also much concerned with matters of text underlay that would ensure a graceful matching of musical and text accent as well as preserve syntactical integrity.[20] Zarlino's rules for matching text and notes in *Le Istitutioni harmoniche* represent stylistic norms of the mid- to late sixteenth century, norms that hold sway even when text underlay in sources is irregular or not explicit, as was certainly sometimes the case. With regard to accentuation, Zarlino suggests: "Over a long or a short syllable put a corresponding note value, so that no barbarism will be heard." That is, accented syllables in the text should be matched with long notes in the music; unaccented ones with short notes. He prescribes that ligatures be melismatic— "no more than one syllable should be assigned to the beginning of a ligature of several notes"—and that syllabic underlay be generally avoided in fast passages: "Generally, one rarely places a syllable under a semiminim or under notes that are smaller than the semiminim." With regard to text repetitions, his concern is with preserving the sense of the words: "[I]n mensural music . . . repetitions [of text] are tolerable; I do not mean repetition of a syllable or word, but repetititon of some part of a text of which the sense is complete." And he continues, noting that too much repetition may prove problematic, unless one is seeking to emphasize certain words.[21]

NOTES

1. In Sally Allis Sanford, "Seventeenth- and Eighteenth-Century Vocal Style and Technique" (DMA diss., Stanford University, 1979), 56–57.

2. In Carol MacClintock, *Readings in the History of Music in Performance* (Bloomington: Indiana University Press, 1979), 69.

3. "Reconstructing Pre-Romantic Singing Technique," in John Potter, *The Cambridge Companion to Singing* (Cambridge: Cambridge University Press, 2000), 186.

4. Sally Sanford, "A Comparison of French and Italian Singing in the Seventeenth Century," *Journal of Seventeenth-Century Music* 1, no. 1 (1995): sect. 7.1, available at www.sscm-jscm.org/jscm.

5. In Jeffrey Kurtzman, *The Monteverdi Vespers of 1610: Music, Context, and Performance* (Oxford: Oxford University Press, 1999), 389.

6. Joseph Dyer, "Singing with Proper Refinement: From *De Modo bene cantandi* by Conrad von Zabern (1474)," *Early Music* 6 (1978): 215.

7. Florence 1602. See Oliver Strunk, *Source Readings in Music History* (New York: W. W. Norton, 1950), 377–78.

8. See, for instance, Girolamo Fantini's description of such an ornament for the trumpet in his 1638 treatise, *Modo per imparare a sonare di tromba*: "It should also be noted that when there are notes of any length, that is, of one, or two, or four beats, they should be held in a cantabile manner, starting with a low sound, then increasing the volume until halfway through the note, and then making a diminuendo right to the end of the beat, which should hardly be heard; for by so doing, perfect harmony will be produced." In Don L. Smithers, *The Music and History of the Baroque Trumpet before 1721* (Carbondale: Southern Illinois University Press, 1988), 84.

9. See Roger North, *Notes of Me,* ed. Peter Millard (Toronto: University of Toronto Press, 2000), 149–50. See also Gable, "Some Observations Concerning Baroque and Modern Vibrato," *Performance Practice Review* 5 (1992): 92.

10. Von Ramm, "Singing Early Music," *Early Music* 4 (1976): 13.

11. Howard Mayer Brown, *Embellishing Sixteenth-Century Music* (London: Oxford University Press, 1976).

12. Diminution practice spawned a large body of didactic literature, catalogued in Ernest T. Ferand, "Didactic Embellishment Literature in the Late Renaissance: A Survey of Sources," in *Aspects of Medieval and Renaissance Music: A Birthday Offering to Gustave Reese,* ed. Jan LaRue (New York: W. W.

Norton, 1966), 154–72. Richard Erig has impressively collected all the surviving examples of pieces with multiple diminutions in his handsome volume, *Italienische Diminutionen* (Zurich: Amadeus Verlag, 1979). Though he has collected written examples, the practice was, in the main, an improvisational one.

13. Nota bene: The suspension in the original [*] is replaced consistently by consonance in the ornamentation [*].

14. In MacClintock, *Readings,* 69–70. Cf. also Zarlino, who rules out choral embellishment, cited by Christopher Reynolds, "Sacred Polyphony," in Brown and Sadie, *Performance Practice,* 196.

15. Cf. Blachly: "The highly competitive arena in which Renaissance singers were traded, bought, and sold should convince us that music making in this period must have been on par with musical composition itself and with the creations of painters, sculptors, and architects, that is, consummately polished and intended to be impressive in every way." "On Singing and the Vocal Ensemble I," in *A Performer's Guide to Renaissance Music,* ed. Jeffery T. Kite-Powell (New York: Schirmer, 1994), 16.

16. From the *Politics,* in *Strunk's Source Readings in Music History,* ed. Leo Treitler (New York, W. W. Norton, 1998), 29.

17. In Treitler, *Source Readings,* 86.

18. *Against the Musicians,* in Treitler, *Source Readings,* 97.

19. Gioseffo Zarlino, *On the Modes: Part Four of Le Istitutioni Harmoniche, 1558,* trans. Vered Cohen (New Haven, Conn.: Yale University Press, 1983), 58, 64, 67, 70, 72, 74, 77, 83, 85, and 86.

20. For a summary of Zarlino's views on music and text, see Don Harrán, *Word-Tone Relations in Musical Thought from Antiquity to the Seventeenth Century* (Neuhausen-Stuttgart: Hänssler-Verlag, 1986), 189–217.

21. Zarlino, *On the Modes,* 98–99.

Chapter 7

Putting Things into Practice

At this point in our discussion, with a large number of ideas and concerns laid before us, it is time to consider practical applications of this material in the form of two test cases: a few movements from the *Missa Pastores quidnam vidistis* by Jacobus [?] Clemens non Papa, published in Leuven in 1559, and the psalm setting, "Jauchzet dem Herren" (SWV 36), by Heinrich Schütz from his *Psalmen Davids* of 1619. Clemens, a Flemish composer in the tradition of Josquin, was active in the north at Bruge, Leiden, and Ypres. Typical of his time, his output is rich in liturgical offerings, including fifteen masses and over two hundred motets. The majority of his masses are examples of the "parody" or "imitation" mass, in which the polyphony of the mass is derived from the polyphony of a preexistent model, be it motet, madrigal, or chanson.[1] Clemens's *Missa pastores* is based, for example, on his own Christmas motet, *Pastores quidnam vidistis.* Schütz (1585–1672) was the Electoral Chapelmaster at Dresden from 1617. A major force in bringing the early Baroque style into blossom, especially in its nonoperatic manifestations, he was much influenced by his studies in Venice with Giovanni Gabrieli and Claudio Monteverdi. His *Psalmen Davids* are large-scale, polychoral psalms that bear the unmistakable stamp of his Venetian study.

CLEMENS—*MISSA PASTORES QUIDNAM VIDISTIS*

Performance Parts and Scores

There are both manuscript and printed sources for the mass from the sixteenth century as well as a modern *Urtext,* critical edition.[2]

Both the modern and the original source material present advantages and challenges to modern singers. The genre of *Urtext* edition is rooted in the rival tug and pull between accessibility on the one hand and fidelity to the original on the other. Ideally these editions, which we associate with collected works and historical sets, contain only minimal editorial intrusion—enough to render it "accessible," but with all editing clearly discernible as such. Modern clefs and note shapes are typical, note values may be proportionally reduced to convey a better sense of speed, ficta may be provided, obvious mistakes corrected, variant readings provided, and single-line sources rendered into score. In general, the modern singer sees nothing here that cannot be read and interpreted, but also finds that, as interpretative, expressive detail was not part of the original notation, it does not figure here either. From the *Urtext*, then, one can usually construct a reasonably clear picture of the original source material, and at the same time view the notation in a familiar style and format.[3]

On the other hand, the original print is in choirbook format with each of the five voice parts in a discrete part of the page; here, on the left-hand verso are, top to bottom, superius 1, superius 2, and tenor; on the right-hand recto are contratenor and bassus. To modern singers, much here is new and potentially challenging, such as the absence of a coordinated score format with its possibility of orientation, the use of unfamiliar clefs (here ct = c2; t = c3; b = c4; the superius parts are in the customary g-clefs), the incompleteness of text underlay (in the Kyrie, for instance, repetitions of the text phrase are simply indicated by a "ii" underneath a collection of notes), the use of breve notation with longer note values that go quicker than their modern equivalents—this requires, as well, the use of rests that get little use in modern notation—and the absence of barlines. The note heads are diamond-shaped equivalents of modern characters that require little, if any, adjustment in and of themselves. Despite those things to which the modern singer will be unaccustomed—and the list does seem formidable—there is much to commend singing from this kind of format, given the time, flexibility, and practical circumstance to pursue it.

Joscelyn Godwin some years ago remarked, "[I]n spite of the contributions of musicologists and instrument makers, who have gone far towards restoring the sounds of the past, today's performer will still have his eyes firmly fixed on the present, if he is playing or singing from a modern edition."[4] Godwin's remark pulls in a number of directions. In part, one suspects, the visual aesthetic of the Renaissance print is resonant with the musical aesthetic of the day, particularly in its ornamental decoration and also, most tellingly, the way that the choirbook format reinforces visually the idea of contrapuntal independence.[5] And in a subliminal way, at least, this unity of visual and aural elements is compelling. The difference between the visual aesthetic of the modern print and its Renaissance counterpart is large, and rather than reinforcing a common aesthetic between sound and image, the modern print may actually challenge it. Certainly the decorated initials of the sixteenth-century print nurture an ornamental expressive sense absent in the sterile spareness of the modern edition, a spareness far removed from the actual sound of the piece, but also a spareness that is resonant with the objective scientificism that forms the foundation of critical editions.

In a more concrete way, the original format does much to encourage freedom of line and rhythmic flexibility, both nurtured by the absence of barlines, whose visual presence can force unintended metrical patterns and fragment the flow of melodic lines. (The modern *Urtext* edition for this piece, as is often the case, adopts the use of *Mensurstriche*, barlines between the staves that offer reference points—you can say "in measure three," for instance—but that keep the staff unimpeded, as in the original.) And the original format presenting one part only, not a score, encourages a radically different aural awareness of ensemble context.

Practical demands and performance pressure may well make the use of original notation an out-of-reach luxury. Even among professional early music vocal ensembles, modern notation remains the rule. However, a middle ground between modern and original formats is compelling. For instance, in working with a group of students, I recently prepared and used the modern equivalents of partbooks for a Palestrina mass to dramatically effective ends. In these partbooks, I employed modern notational figures and modern clefs, but provided no *musica ficta*, no barlines, no ties, and only limited text underlay. In an informal rehearsal, we learned the notes reasonably quickly (there were no notational characters that would have been unfamiliar); with notes learned, we then began to sing with everybody beating the slow, organizing tactus. This quickly encouraged more flow because it reduced the number of beats that a modern singer might typically bring to the writing—fewer subdivisions.

The next step was to have everyone beat the tactus on a neighbor's shoulder while singing. This became a remarkable prod to ensemble cohesion. The beating of the tactus itself had nurtured flow and shape; the beating of the tactus for one another transformed that flow and shape into a dancelike, shared concept. One singer, as I recall, remarked, "I'm singing what you're moving."

In this modern partbook session, the absence of a score format meant that motivic memory was on high alert. For example, if one needed to make an entry after a rest, especially one of some duration, one engaged as a reference point earlier versions of the motive that one had already sung. Pitch became self-referential, with the added bonus that one began to listen to pitch in a newly attentive way—of necessity. To know on what pitch to enter, one had to remember the sound of reference notes. Moreover, and perhaps ironically, singing with only one's own part before one seemed also to heighten the aural awareness of the other voices that one did not see, as if freed of the sight of them, the ear could attend to them with greater sensitivity. Certainly the students sang with a greater sense of aural awareness and more integration of the parts.

Having done all of this, I then gave them the mass movement in a modern score version and asked them to sing it anew. It was striking how square and relatively constrained it sounded; the lines moved slowly and heavily. One student commented, "it sounds like it looks!" With the score before them, the students found it difficult not to keep checking out references to the other parts visually, and this seemed to lessen their aural sense of the music. Undoubtedly, they sang it much better without a score.

As an experiment, it proved most enlightening. Is it a practical solution? It *does* require a good bit of time to prepare the parts from which to sing, and rehearsing is sometimes made awkward by the absence of common reference points—for example, if the singing breaks down and you want to fix it, from where do you start? There are no bar numbers. But by the same token, there were no hurdles of sophistication required to access and navigate the parts—no unfamiliar note heads, no unfamiliar clefs, etc. And the gains seemed significant, indeed.

With the Clemens mass at hand, then, one has the choice of original formats, modern *Urtext* edition, or a self-prepared middle ground between them. Certainly these are the choices that much of the Renaissance repertory presents. At the same time, modern performance editions of Renaissance music are by no means rare, and they invite special care by the performer.

In this type of edition, admittedly much rarer now than a few generations ago, the editorial intrusion into the text of the work itself may be extensive, and, misleadingly, may not be consistently identified as editorial. Thus, one of the chief difficulties of these once popular choral octavos is that items of interpretative discretion appear as items invested with textual authority, inviting the performer's dutiful response. Once the genre of edition has been identified, one may, of course, be well-positioned to know what to ignore or to evaluate more closely, but distractingly, this requires learning what *not* to see, as well as what to see. An expressive crescendo of some sort *may* prove stylistically effective in some sixteenth-century contexts, but for an editor to insert it as part of the text—certainly a notational anachronism—imposes a narrower range of interpretation and invites the performer to view the gesture as an obligation. One may knowingly figure out what is editorial and what is not, but the energy and visual distraction involved in ignoring such things may be vexing.

Performance Pitch

In determining the pitch level at which one will perform, one needs to have one eye on the historical evidence of the sources and the other on the practicalities of the present circumstance. Which eye claims the more privileged view is, of course, one of the engaging variables of interpretation. As mentioned above, the clef configuration in the original is superius 1 = g2; superius 2 = g2; tenor = c3; contratenor = c2; and bass = c4. This is close to the traditional "high clef" configuration (the only distinction being here the bass in tenor clef instead of baritone clef [f3]), with the implication that things should be transposed down a fourth or fifth.

For modern choirs, the contratenor line is problematically too low for female altos, though quite comfortable for tenors. In making a transposed version fit the modern mixed choir, then, one might well combine female sopranos and altos on each of the superius lines. This would be preferred to giving the second superius to the altos alone because this would cause a striking timbral distinction between parts whose range, motives, and style are essentially equal. Thus a transposed, modern choir version might effectively be

superius 1 = soprano and alto
superius 2 = soprano and alto
contratenor = tenor
tenor = baritone
bass = bass
bass 2 [Agnus] = bass

If swayed by the practicality of performing it at written pitch, the configuration of s s a t b would work, and in addition to the issues of practicality, one would gain a timbral brightness that might prove attractive in a Christmas mass. This "modern" configuration could also be used with a modest downward transposition that would prevent the basses from singing frequent high d's in the Agnus, though admittedly, one would buy their ease at the loss of the altos' bottom range.

The Performance Ensemble

As discussed above, the composition of contemporaneous ensembles was variable, not unlike their modern counterparts, and variety of performance context in both the Renaissance and the present day is surely a significant influence. Size of room, nature of the occasion, questions of audience, etc., all will and did help shape ensemble decisions. Presumably, the chosen quantity of performers is, in itself, potentially impressive. For example, one of the grandest of occasions in cinquecento Italy was surely the celebration of the wedding of Ferdinand de' Medici to Christine of Lorraine in Florence in 1589. Lavish intermedii to accompany Bargagli's *La Pellegrina* brought together a number of composers, and the final ballo by Cavalieri was performed by a staggering number of performers: sixty singers and between twenty and twenty-five instrumentalists.[6] The occasion called for the glory of the Medici to be reflected in the performance and propagated in performance accounts, and clearly the scale of the performance contributed hugely to that. Admittedly, questions of genre and context may skew the comparison to the Clemens mass, but the notion of scale as a performance factor seems indisputable.

Accordingly then, given the high rank of Christmas within the liturgical calendar, one might opt for a certain grandeur of means. However, much evidence shows, as indicated in chapter 3, that one-to-a-part singing was quite normal in ensemble circumstances in a variety of contexts.

The source material for Clemens's mass offers some clues that for much of the work, more than one-to-a-part was used here. For example, certain sections[7] are denominated as "TRIO," an indication perhaps less of the fact that it contains three vocal lines—this seems self-evident—than that the three lines might be sung by a "trio," that is, solo singers. Also suggestive that much of the polyphony was sung by more than solo singers is the addition of a sixth voice, a second bass, in the final movement, the Agnus Dei. If the mass were being performed by a solo ensemble, this would require a single singer to be on hand for just this one movement, a relatively brief one at that, and while it is possible that that was the case, it seems to go against a commonsensical view. As a Christmas work, as well, one may easily imagine the deployment of the fullest chapel resources for a performance of the work, and that might well suggest doubled voices, too. Thus, liturgical context, descriptive labeling in the printed source, and the expansion of the number of voice parts at the work's end are all suggestive, though scarcely conclusive, of a performance with more than solo singers. And following the line of thought that the liturgical occasion would elicit display, one might also well imagine the doubling of voices by instruments, *colla parte*.

The traditional doubling instruments of cornetts and trombones could well be deployed here. In general, if one opts for instrumental doubling, the concept of the instrumental-vocal mix as the pervading timbre is best maintained, and attempts at an "orchestrated," selective use of the instruments may lead to fragmentation rather than enrichment. That said, however, there are places where the deletion of doubling instruments seems either called for—the solo trio sections, for instance—or expressively affective, as in the "halo" sections, the *suscipe deprecationem nostram* in the Gloria or the *et homo factus est* section in the Credo. Here, slower rhythms and more homophonic textures suggest an intended reverential special effect, and the sudden cessation of the instruments at these points sensitively underscores the gesture.

Performance Details—The Kyrie and Gloria

Kyrie Eleison

The Kyrie is notated with a slashed C time signature, indicating a breve tactus; thus, in the *Urtext* edition, a slow, organizing pulse of one-to-a-bar. However, the tempo of breve = 60 MM seems hurried, given the number of semiminims (eighths in the edition) and also the richness of the suspension dissonances. Thus the slashed C here more appropriately seems to suggest the unit of beat and groupings rather than an objective, fixed speed. A more relaxed speed also accords well with the penitential nature of the text. The consideration of textual affection is often a sound guide, but in this case something of a slippery slope to climb, because of the mass's close (and aurally obvious) relationship to the parent motet, "Pastores quidnam," whose affection would be strikingly different.

The rhythms of the Kyrie are delightfully independent of metric constraints and abound in interesting cross-rhythms among the parts. For example, the opening motive (see ex. 7.1) introduces a triple grouping against a duple measure, and interestingly, as the first sounds of the piece are of the triple pattern alone, the notion of a duple-measure background emerges only gradually with the tenor entry in the third bar, an ambiguity of meter that creates considerable interest. The opening of the third Kyrie also features much ametrical rhythmical freedom (see ex. 7.2). Edited with visual orientation to the tactus, the parts will look like an entry "off the beat"; special care must be taken then that the first notes of the motives feel like true downbeats. However, seen without barlines or their editorial surrogates, *Mensurstriche*, there is no temptation to treat the lower voice, imitative entries as syncopations (see ex. 7.3). As discussed in chapter 5, text underlay *can* be helpful in clarifying the accentual scheme. Ideally, accents of the text will coincide with accents in the music, regardless of metrical background. Text underlay, however, can be quite variable. In this case, the original print and manuscript sources of the Kyrie are only inexactly underlaid. Regardless, it is easy to fit the text to the triple rhythm. The motet on which the mass is based shows a decidedly less felicitous arrangement (see ex. 7.4). Here, the weak last syllable of *Pastores* is stressed by both its coincidence with a leap to a high note and, following the triple rhythms, a rhythmically strong position.

Example 7.1.   Clemens non Papa, *Missa Pastores quidnam vidistis*—Kyrie (mm. 1-5)

Example 7.2.   Clemens non Papa, *Missa Pastores quidnam vidistis*—Kyrie (mm. 59-67)

Example 7.3.   Clemens non Papa, *Missa Pastores quidnam vidistis*—Kyrie Motives

Example 7.4.   Clemens non Papa, "Pastores quidnam vidistis" (*Cantio Sacra*)

Underlay, where possible, may need to be adjusted for a better match of accent. Also, as in some sources the text underlay has not been carefully applied, one will want to consider making it uniform from part to part, especially in imitative textures.

In the opening point (see ex. 7.1), issues of stress take on other manifestations, as well. For instance, the b-flat downbeat of the third measure in the superius is an important note because it is the first downbeat after duple grouping has taken over, and moreover, its half-step tension with the "a" gives it a strong gravitational pull. In shaping the passage, then, one will want to take all of this into account. Singing the b-flat on the low side will enhance its gravitational tension—its tendency to resolve downward—and leaning on the b-flat will further enhance that character. Although this leaning can be accomplished by attack, it is more effectively done with expressive shaping of the note. A swell-and-taper shaping, even on a semibreve if the context makes it important, can be a helpful, clarifying gesture.

In terms of clarifying the rhythm, as well, articulation plays a very strong role. The opening triple motive, for instance, is more effectively perceived as such not by attack and accent on the strong beats, but by discrete articulation before the strong beats, employing either a glottal stroke or space between notes, as example 7.5 suggests.

Example 7.5. Clemens non Papa, *Missa Pastores quidnam vidistis*—Kyrie

Articulation becomes important subsequently, as well, toward the end of the section. Ornamental passing notes, as in example 7.6, will require glottal articulation, not slurring, though as usual, the articulation should not impede a sense of line. To enhance shape and contour of these figures it is helpful to reduce them to their background content and then gradually to introduce the notes of lesser importance, as illustrated in example 7.7.

Example 7.6. Clemens non Papa, *Missa Pastores quidnam vidistis*—Kyrie (mm. 15-16)

Example 7.7. Rehearsal of bass figure (see ex. 7.6)

Gloria in excelsis deo

The Gloria polyphonically begins with the second phrase of its text. Accordingly, for liturgical propriety as well as for the integrity of the text, it is necessary to provide a chant incipit for the first phrase. The *Liber usualis* provides a number of possibilities in its collection of chants for the Ordinary, the choice of which is governed by mode, melodic compatibility, and liturgical aptness. Transposition of the incipit may be necessary to achieve these ends.

The beginning of the Gloria introduces the same degree of ametrical freedom that was seen in the Kyrie. Elsewhere, however, the
meter reinforces the groupings, as in example 7.8. Articulation that
gives a trace of space between *Lau* and *da* is important in reinforcing
this, and a liquid, springy *l* and ample attention to the diphthong of
Lau will nicely shape this pickup and keep it from being too short.

Example 7.8.   Clemens non Papa, *Missa Pastores quidnam vidistis*—**Gloria (mm.
13-14)**

Clemens uses repeated notes to add clarity to his text, as at the
Gratias agimus tibi. The tenor's opening version of the motive is well-
conceived with all three *d*'s antecedent in feel: a collective pickup
figure (see ex. 7.9). And the maintenance of this anacrusic sense of
the repeated notes throughout the exposition of this motive keeps
awkward metrical accents from occurring.

Example 7.9.   Clemens non Papa, *Missa Pastores quidnam vidistis*—**Gloria (mm.
24-25)**

The *Domine fili* not only shows the typical ametrical freedom but
also places it in an engaging context of cross-rhythms. As before, the
most effective way to mark the triplet is not with attack, but rather
with articulative space after the third note of the triplet. In addition,
the accent on *"Do-"* is aided by the length of the note and invites a
tapered shape (see ex. 7.10).

Example 7.10. Clemens non Papa, *Missa Pastores quidnam vidistis*—Gloria (mm. 49-53)

The text of the Gloria is diverse, ranging from jubilant praise to supplicative tones. It is likely, I think, that extreme and extensive contrast in the service of this range is not particularly at home in this aesthetic, particularly when one considers the often uniform texture and contrapuntal procedures. However, at the gestural, localized level, dynamic contrast can be most effective. In Clemens's setting of the phrase *suscipe deprecationem nostram*, the sudden homophony is a stunning effect after so much counterpoint; that is, it is set apart gesturally. One might then undergird the sense of gesture with a dynamic contrast of soft singing here, or as mentioned above, the withdrawal of doubling instruments.

Such gestures do show the capacity for a basically uniform technique to respond to affective particularities in the text and, in so doing, to give a section its own character. The brilliance of the final *in gloria Dei Patris Amen* (see ex. 7.11) is a particularly splendid instance, and certainly a climactic end to the movement, characterized by suddenly faster motion and a change to triplets with complex interaction between the parts, including hemiola relationships. The print indicates slashed C3 here, tripling the speed of the opening slashed C. Thus sb sb = sb sb sb sb sb sb. This ending to the movement is exuberant and highly rhythmicized, and it is a good example of how the music itself supplies much of the climactic substance. Dramatically climactic means of performance then are in a sense superogative.

Example 7.11. Clemens non Papa, *Missa Pastores quidnam vidistis*—Gloria (mm. 160–164)

SCHÜTZ—"JAUCHZET DEM HERREN"

Performance Parts and Scores

The *Psalmen Davids* were originally published in partbooks, not in score. By way of contrast to the Clemens mass above, however, the relation of the parts one to another is frequently homophonic, at least within each of its two, four-voice choirs, and thus a modern score format reinforces the nature of the polyphony, rather than veils it: That which sounds together is written together, and thus the score format becomes a visual metaphor of the homophonic textures. From this standpoint, then, performance from a modern edition is unproblematic.[8] Moreover, as the music moves with metrical clarity and directness, the use of modern bar lines (as in the basso continuo part of the original print) is also unproblematic.

Performance Pitch

The notated pitch of the original appears low to modern expectations: a low "a" in a soprano part, and a low "f" in both alto and bass. In mixed gender ensembles, the depth of the soprano and alto parts, then, will inevitably present challenges, and practicality seems to argue for an upward transposition.[9] Historical circumstance, on the other hand, does not. As Bruce Haynes has recently underscored, Venetian pitch "set the standard in the countries of Europe" in the sixteenth and seventeenth centuries, in part an acknowledgment of Venice's premier status in the manufacture of woodwind instruments.[10] The most common pitch in Venice at the end of the sixteenth century was the *mezzo punto*, a pitch level that, based on surviving cornetti, averages A = 466 Hz, that is, around a half step higher than modern pitch. However, on the other hand, the pitch level known as the *tuono corista*, as its name implies a "choir pitch," was generally a whole step lower than *mezzo punto*. This is also reinforced by Praetorius, whose *Chor Thon* (choir pitch) and *Cammer Thon* (chamber pitch for instruments) is analogous to the Italian *tuono corista* and *mezzo punto*.[11] Thus, historical circumstance would seem to suggest a pitch standard one half step below modern pitch. Bridging the distance between practicality and history is, of course, an interpretative matter. In this case, however, it is an interpretative matter that is much influenced by the makeup of the ensemble, mixed gender or all-male.

The Performance Ensemble

"Jauchzet dem Herren" is written for two four-voiced ensembles (SATB) with basso continuo, the second choir being an echo to the first, as the heading in the basso continuo part makes explicit: *Eccho a' 8.* The vocal forces could fruitfully be both choral or one-to-a-part. However, given the specific reference to echo, a choral choir 1 with a solo choir 2 is highly effective. This version of the echo effect, that is, the contrast of choral and solo forces, would also have the advantage of allowing the second choir to be sung with full voices, resonant with the jubilant affection of the text, rather than requiring it to be sung in a dynamically constrained manner by a larger ensemble.

Instrumental doubling of the voices, especially given the jubilant nature of the text and its specific gesture of inclusivity ("Jauchzet dem Herren *alle Welt"*), is well employed here, and admits of several possibilities. Each choir could be doubled by a homogeneous consort—trombones and cornett for the *coro proposta* (choir 1), for instance, and a violin consort for the *coro riposta* (choir 2), the latter timbre being of a softer quality than that of the brasses and thus enhancing the echo effect. Alternatively, the instrumental doubling could be reserved for the first choir alone, thus maximizing elements of contrast between the forces.

The continuo ensemble also invites a variety of approaches. One continuist could play a *basso seguente* realization, combining the bass lines of each choir into one structural part. This is a particularly workable solution if the two choirs are placed in close proximity to each other. On the other hand, spatial displacement of the choirs to any significant degree will require a continuo instrument for each choir. It is clear that physical separation of antiphonal choirs was part of Schütz's performance practice. For example, the prefatory material to his polychoral German Magnificat makes specific reference to two facing galleries as a venue for the work's performance.[12] It is possible, however, that the contemporary tradition of this polychoral repertory has exaggerated the importance of spatial separation. James Moore offers an important corrective, noting that in the Basilica of San Marco—in the modern view, the temple of polychoralism—multiple choirs sang antiphonal music from one unified space—a platform to the right of the iconostasis—not from the separated choir galleries:

> [A] point that must be re-examined is the placement of musicians for *salmi spezzati.* The structure mentioned most often in the documents is, surprisingly enough, not the choirlofts, but an octagonal platform on the floor of the church called the *bigonzo* or "tub," the very structure drawn by Canaletto in his famous sketch of the singers of St. Mark's.[13]

As in many other performance matters, historical circumstance presents a range of choice.

Performance Details

The opening triple meter phrase (see ex. 7.12) is effectively performed in a one-to-the-bar, dancelike motion corresponding to the unit of one tactus. In achieving a buoyant lilt, attention to contour and stress is crucial. Example 7.12 illustrates the succession of strong and weak beats, the use of articulative space before primary accents, and the shaping of long notes—all factors that invest the motive with character and contour.

Example 7.12. Schütz, "Jauchzet dem Herren"—opening motive (soprano)

Rehearsing a reduced, background version and gradually adding the notes of the full motive is, once again, an effective way of achieving contour and flow, as illustrated in example 7.13.

Example 7.13. Schütz, "Jauchzet dem Herren"—opening motive rehearsed

This same principle of reduction will also help shape passages like the melismatic "Amen," where the tendency may be amid the many notes to introduce too many beats, and as a result, mask the simple, strong-weak, two-to-the-bar feeling of the tactus. Thus, as example 7.14 illustrates, the flow and contour is shaped by the slow tactus, not the subdivisions, and may be rehearsed accordingly. Faster notes should receive glottal articulation, but at the same time an articulation that promotes fluidity and shape.

Example 7.14. Schütz, "Jauchzet dem Herren"—Amen (bass)

The melismatic ending is ornamental, and that in itself may suggest ornamental additions in other places, especially in the context of repetition between the choirs. Example 7.15 illustrates one representative way in which static repetition may be enlivened with the addition of ornamental passage work, as described in chapter 6.

Example 7.15.   Schütz, "Jauchzet dem Herren"—repetitions with added embellishment

The ornamental additions are soloistic, not generally for choral use, but in performances combining choral and solo forces, the addition of ornamental divisions by the solo choir not only enhances the feeling of dynamism but also considerably heightens the elements of contrast. Moreover, ornamental divisions might well be played by instrumentalists in their doubling of the vocal lines.

One of the expressive high points of the motet is the section devoted to the text "Denn der Herr ist freundlich," set apart by long note values and the cessation of the typical rhythmic activity (see ex. 7.16).

Example 7.16.   Schütz, "Jauchzet dem Herren"

One might fruitfully have this passage rendered by voices alone—no *colla parte* instrumentation—as a way of underscoring its special effect. This would further be enhanced by a finely contoured swell and decay on the syllable "freund-."

The two examples treated here, a mid-sixteenth-century contrapuntal mass setting and an early seventeenth-century antiphonal psalm, present a number of performance issues that are typical of their respective genres and historical contexts. Ametrical rhythmic freedom, for instance, is a nearly constant part of the sixteenth-century contrapuntal style; ornamental repetition is a frequent interpretative choice in early seventeenth-century repertories, etc. Each genre and style has its own idiosyncrasies. It is striking, however, that even across genre and historical circumstance, certain issues here are pressing ones. In both the Clemens mass and the Schütz psalm, for example, we see the need to be alert to the integrity of the slower rhythmic layers, to choose speeds that render the tactus intelligible, and to develop phrasing that emphasizes its roots in that background rhythmic layer. Similarly, both works are enhanced by a focus on contour, not only at the level of the phrase, but more particularly in the shaping of long notes. The general absence of "square-shaped" notes of any significant length not only invests the lines with naturalness but also heightens their expressivity. The preceding discussions have been based in part on the notion that a generalized, monolithic "early music style" is as difficult to formulate as it is unfruitful to embrace. However, these issues of contour and rhythmic integrity seem to assert themselves with a frequency that, if short of being hallmarks of "the" early style, nevertheless suggests they are highly idiomatic elements in much premodern performance.

NOTES

1. For a discussion of the concept of *imitatio* in Renaissance music, see Howard Mayer Brown, "Emulation, Competition, and Homage: Imitation and Theories of Imitation in the Renaissance," *Journal of the American Musicological Society* 35 (1982): 1–48.

2. The original print, *Missa cum quinque vocibus ad imitationem moduli, Pastores quidnam vidistis . . .* was published by Pierre Phalese in Leuven in 1559;

E Mn M2431 presents a manuscript version. (I am grateful tó Douglas Kirk of Montreal for providing a photocopy of portions of this source.) The modern critical edition is *Jacobus Clemens non Papa: Opera Omnia*, in *Corpus Mensurabilis Musicae*, ed. K. Ph. Bernet Kempers ([n.p.]: American Institute of Musicology, 1959), VI.

3. On editing and types of edition, see Philip Brett, "Text, Context, and the Early Music Editor," in *Authenticity and Early Music: A Symposium*, ed. Nicholas Kenyon (London: Oxford University Press, 1988), 83–114.

4. "Playing from Original Notation," *Early Music* 2 (1974): 15.

5. Tellingly, some of the earliest examples of score notation are associated with homophonic textures whose unanimity is reinforced by the visual coordination on the page. See, for example, the music of the Old Hall Manuscript where continentally influenced, contrapuntal pieces retain the traditional partbook format, but the novel English discant, in homophonic style, is rendered in score.

6. See F. W. Sternfeld, "Aspects of Italian Intermedi and Early Opera," in *Convivium musicorum: Festschrift Wolfgang Boetticher zum sechzigsten Geburtstag am 19 August 1974* (Berlin: Verlag Merseburger, 1974), 363. For accounts of the Florentine intermedi see, inter alia, Howard Mayer Brown, *Sixteenth-Century Instrumentation: The Music for the Florentine Intermedi* ([n.p.]: American Institute of Musicology, 1973); and A. M. Nagler, *Theatre Festivals of the Medici, 1534–1637*, trans. George Hickenlooper (New Haven, Conn.: Yale University Press, 1964).

7. See for example, "Domine deus" [Gloria] (tenor, contratenor, and bassus), "Et resurrexit" [Credo] (superius 1, superius 2, and contratenor), "Benedictus" [Sanctus] (tenor, contratenor, and bassus).

8. See, for example, Heinrich Schütz, *Psalmen Davids 1619 Nr. 10–16*, in *Neue Ausgabe Sämtlicher Werke*, ed. Wilhelm Ehmann (Kassel: Bärenreiter, 1979), vol. 24.

9. The Ehmann edition transposes the motet up one whole step, to good effect.

10. See *A History of Performing Pitch: The Story of "A"* (Lanham, Md.: Scarecrow Press, 2002), 58.

11. *A History of Performing Pitch*, 65, 76.

12. See *Psalmen Davids*, vol. 24, XV.

13. James H. Moore, "The *Vespro delle Cinque Laudate* and the Role of *Salmi Spezzati* at St. Mark's," *Journal of the American Musicological Society* 34 (1981): 277.

Chapter 8

So What?

Many years ago I read for the first time a passage by Pontus de Tyard (1555) describing the magical playing of the Italian lute virtuoso, Francesco da Milano. Though in part the description seems a familiar trope on the powers of Orpheus—all sit with rapt attention to a great musician as their affections are moved by the music—the passage remains memorable to me for what it seems to say about the intentionality of the act of performance. It appears that Francesco's playing is not only commanding, but that Francesco *commands*; it appears that Francesco's playing is not only moving, but that Francesco *moves* his hearers.

The passage recounts a dinner party attended by Monsieur de Ventemille in Milan, and appearing among the guests is Francesco,

> a man who is considered to have attained the end (if such is possible) of perfection in playing the lute well. The tables being cleared, he chose one, and as if tuning his strings, sat on the end of a table seeking out a fantasia. He had barely disturbed the air with three strummed chords when he interrupted conversation which had started among the guests. Having constrained them to face him, he continued with such a ravishing skill that little by little, making the strings languish under his fingers in his sublime way, he transported all those who were listening into so pleasurable a melancholy that . . . they remained deprived of all senses save that of hearing, as if the spirit, having abandoned all the seats of the senses, had retired to the ears in order to enjoy the more at its ease so ravishing a harmony; and I believe that we would be there still, had he not himself—I know not how—changing his style of playing with a gentle force, returned the spirit and the

senses to the place from which he had stolen them, not without leav-
ing as much astonishment in each of us as if we had been elevated by
an ecstatic transport of some divine frenzy.[1]

What seems memorable here is the agency—the affects are not casual by-products of music, but rather the fruits of an intentional act
by the performer. And this intentionality would seem to suggest a
high degree of engagement by performer and audience alike. It may
also suggest a high degree of individuality, for it is *Francesco* who
does this, not lutanists in general. Moreover, that this takes place in
circumstances where the music might have reasonably been more
social than artistically engaging—Francesco is there presumably to
provide dinner music—makes this all the more remarkable.

How might this relate to our interest in Renaissance choral performance? Was high engagement the norm in Renaissance choral
music? Were Renaissance vocal ensembles the purveyors of generic,
conventionalized style, or highly interpreted acts? Does conventionalized style preclude interpretation, or is it rather the language
through which interpretation is mediated? It is hard to peel back the
curtain of time and place and view the historical mentality of performance. Certainly the contexts in which the music was performed
are suggestive, though as with the Francesco example, not always
true to expectation. In the repertory that has most concerned us
here—Renaissance liturgical music—the constraints of the liturgical
setting are significant, for they encourage and nurture tradition and
continuity; they exist within a strong communal identity. One might
suspect, then, that a Renaissance mass in situ was not generally an
exercise in individuality or that it invited highly interpreted renditions. The one would run counter to the communal nature of the
liturgy and the other would run counter to the sense of liturgy *including its manner of rendition* as fundamentally part of a continuum.
One's humbling relationship within that continuum might also have
kept individualism at bay.

However, if context leads us in one direction, the spirit of the
times may lead us in another. As long ago as the middle of the nineteenth century, historians of the Renaissance have underscored a
characteristic individualism. Jacob Burckhardt (1860), for instance,
devotes a substantial portion of his monumental *The Civilization of
the Renaissance in Italy* precisely to the development of the individual and the cultivation of the modern sense of fame. He writes:

In the Middle Ages both sides of human consciousness—that which was turned within as that which was turned without—lay dreaming or half awake beneath a common veil. The veil was woven of faith, illusion, and childish prepossession, through which the world and history were seen clad in strange hues. Man was conscious of himself only as member of a race, people, party, family, or corporation—only through some general category. In Italy this veil first melted into air; an *objective* treatment and consideration of the State and of all the things of this world became possible. The *subjective* side at the same time asserted itself with corresponding emphasis; man became a spiritual *individual,* and recognized himself as such.[2]

Moreover, the notion of a heightened subjectivity emerges in various forms of sixteenth-century piety, such as the *Spiritual Exercises* of Ignatius of Loyola, bringing deeply personal, individualized experience into the communal realm of the church where we might not have otherwise expected it.

Thus tradition, continuity, and community in the Renaissance seem to coexist in a creative tension with individualism and subjective experience. And it is in this creative tension that we find a compelling answer to the question "so what?," for in performing this music in the modern day, we cannot avoid the claims of so dynamic a rivalry.

Much of this study has been devoted to clarifying conventions of performance. If the notated page of music is, in essence, an encoded page, it is largely a knowledge of conventions that allows us to decipher the code, to translate the composer's shorthand into expectations of sound that we then, as interpreters, choose to meet in varied ways. The notated symbol on the page represents an expectation of sound. In the very narrowest sense, the note on the staff is an expectation of a certain pitch, but it is only a short step then to ask, what tone quality is expected in that pitch? What sound production is expected for that pitch? What expressive gestures accompany that pitch? How many are expected to produce that pitch? And so forth. Understanding these expectations and their relative claims—not all expectations of sound will have the same priority—is much a matter of understanding the varied traditions in which the work took shape. To proceed with a blind eye and a deaf ear to these traditions is to remove the performance act from vital connections and to isolate the performer in the present, where the language of the code remains a foreign one. Carried to its extreme, the performer deaf to the conventions of tradition will perforce be an interpreter of a work in only its narrowest dimensions.

Interpretation, however, is an act driven by choices, *individual* choices that reflect subjective experience, artistic intent, and circumstance. If much of this study has dealt with conventions, it has also sought to maximize choice, to underscore the inherent variability of historical performance, and to offer an expanded range of performer options for the modern choralist. The partnership between performer and composer in the act of performance is one whose balance has often been reformulated from one historical paradigm to another. Certainly one of the now much-touted attractions of early repertories is the abundant responsibility given to the performer for essential creative choices, choices that in later repertories are more fully under the control of the composer. The conventions of history then not only clarify the expectations of sound but also enshrine the element of choice in dealing with those expectations. Individualism and tradition, though contrary in orientation, meet in a creative, interpretative act that on the one hand goes beyond mere rendition, and on the other, moves beyond exaggerated self-indulgence. The relationship between individualism and tradition then becomes rather contrapuntal and dialogic, like much of the music we have considered. It is a counterpoint well worth savoring in the end.

NOTES

1. *Solitaire second ou prose de la musique* (1555), in H. Colin Slim, "Francesco da Milano (1497–1543/44): A Biographical and Bibliographical Study, I," in *Musica Disciplina* 18 (1964): 79–80.

2. *The Civilization of the Renaissance in Italy* (New York: Harper Colophon, 1958), I, 143.

Bibliography

Ardran, G. M., and David Wulstan. "The Alto or Countertenor Voice." *Music & Letters* 48 (1967): 17–22.

Arnold, F. T. *The Art of Accompaniment from a Thoroughbass as Practiced in the XVIIth & XVIIIth Centuries.* New York: Dover (1965).

Bank, J. A. *Tactus, Tempo, and Notation in Mensural Music from the 13th to the 17th Century.* Amsterdam: Annie Bank, 1972.

Berger, Karol. *Musica Ficta: Theories of Accidental Inflections in Vocal Polyphony. . . .* Cambridge: Cambridge University Press, 1987.

Berman, Morris. *Coming to Our Senses: Body and Spirit in the Hidden History of the West.* New York: Bantam, 1989.

Blachly, Alexander. "Mensuration and Tempo in 15th-Century Music." Ph.D. diss., Columbia University, 1995.

Bonge, Dale. "Gaffurius on Pulse and Tempo: A Reinterpretation." *Musica Disciplina* 36 (1982): 167–74.

Borges, Jose Luis. "Pierre Menard, Author of the Quixote." In *Labyrinths.* New York: New Directions, [1986].

Boudreaux, Margaret Anne. "Michael Praetorius; 'Polyhymnia caduceatrix et panegyrica' (1619): An Annotated Translation." DMA diss., University of Colorado, 1989.

Boulez, Pierre. "The Vestal Virgin and the Fire-stealer: Memory, Creation and Authenticity." *Early Music* 18 (1990): 355–58.

Bowers, Roger. "An 'Aberration' Reviewed: The Reconciliation of Inconsistent Clef-Systems in Monteverdi's Mass and Vespers of 1610." *Early Music* 31 (2003): 527–38.

———. "The Performing Pitch of English 15th-c. Church Polyphony." *Early Music* 8 (1980): 21–28.

Bray, Roger. "More Light on Early Tudor Pitch." *Early Music* 8 (1980): 35–42.

Brown, Howard Mayer. "Choral Music in the Renaissance." *Early Music* 6 (1978): 164–81.

———. *Embellishing Sixteenth-Century Music.* London: Oxford University Press, 1976.

———. "Emulation, Competition, and Homage: Imitation and Theories of Imitation in the Renaissance." *Journal of the American Musicological Society* 35 (1982): 1–48.

———. *Sixteenth-Century Instrumentation: The Music for the Florentine Intermedi.* [n.p.]: American Institute of Musicology, 1973.

Brown, Howard Mayer, and Stanley Sadie, eds. *Performance Practice: Music before 1600.* New York: W. W. Norton, 1990.

Bukofzer, Manfred. "The Beginnings of Choral Polyphony." In *Studies in Medieval and Renaissance Music.* New York: W. W. Norton, 1950.

Burckhardt, Jacob. *The Civilization of the Renaissance in Italy.* New York: Harper Colophon, 1958.

Butt, John. *Playing with History.* Cambridge: Cambridge University Press, 2002.

Clark, J. Bunker. *Transposition in Seventeenth-Century English Organ Accompaniments and the Transposing Organ.* Detroit: Information Coordinators, 1974.

D'Accone, Frank. "The Performance of Sacred Music in Italy during Josquin's Time, c. 1474–1525." In *Proceedings of the International Josquin Festival Conference,* edited by Edward E. Lowinsky. Oxford: Oxford University Press, 1976.

Dixon, Graham. "The Performance of Palestrina: Some Questions, but Fewer Answers." *Early Music* 22 (1994): 666–75.

Dreyfus, Laurence. "Early Music Defended against Its Devotees." *Musical Quarterly* 69 (1983): 297–322.

Duffin, Ross W., ed. *A Performer's Guide to Medieval Music.* Bloomington: Indiana University Press, 2000.

———. "National Pronunciation of Latin ca. 1490–1600." *Journal of Musicology* 4 (1985–1986): 217–26.

Dyer, Joseph. "Singing with Proper Refinement: From *De Modo bene cantandi* by Conrad von Zabern (1474)." *Early Music* 6 (1978): 207–27.

Ehmann, Wilhelm. "Was gut auf Posaunen ist, etc." *Zeitschrift für Musikwissenschaft* 17 (1935): 171–75.

Fallows, David. "The Performing Ensembles in Josquin's Sacred Music." *Tijdschrift van de Vereniging voor Nederlandse Muziekgeschiedenis* 35, nos. 1/2 (1985): 32–64.

Ferand, Ernest T. "Didactic Embellishment Literature in the late Renaissance: A Survey of Sources." In *Aspects of Medieval and Renaissance Music: A Birthday Offering to Gustave Reese,* edited by Jan LaRue. New York: W. W. Norton, 1966.

Gable, Frederick. "Some Observations Concerning Baroque and Modern Vibrato." *Performance Practice Review* 5 (1992): 90–102.

———. "St. Gertrude's Chapel, Hamburg, and the Performance of Polychoral Music." *Early Music* 15 (1987): 229–41.

Garreton, Robert. "The Falsettists." *Choral Journal* 24, no. 1 (1983): 5–7.

Giles, Peter. *The History and Technique of the Countertenor.* Aldershot, England: Scolar Press, 1994.

Godwin, Joscelyn. "Playing from Original Notation." *Early Music* 2 (1974): 15–19.

Handler, Richard, and Eric Gable. *The New History in an Old Museum: Creating the Past at Colonial Williamsburg.* Durham, N.C.: Duke University Press, 1974.

Harrán, Don. "Directions to Singers in Writings of the Early Renaissance." *Revue Belge de Musicologie* 41 (1987): 45–61.

———. *Word-Tone Relations in Musical Thought from Antiquity to the Seventeenth Century.* Neuhausen-Stuttgart, Germany: Hänssler-Verlag, 1986.

Haskell, Harry. *The Early Music Revival: A History.* London: Thames & Hudson, 1988.

Haynes, Bruce. *A History of Performing Pitch: The Story of "A."* Lanham, Md.: Scarecrow Press, 2002.

Heriot, Angus. *The Castrati in Opera.* London: Secker and Warburg, 1956; reprint, 1975.

Hodgson, Frederic. "The Contemporary Alto." *Musical Times* 106 (1965): 293–94.

———. "The Countertenor." *Musical Times* 106 (1965): 216–17.

Johnston, Gregory S. "Polyphonic Keyboard Accompaniment in the Early Baroque: An Alternative to Basso Continuo." *Early Music* 26 (1998): 51–64.

Johnstone, Andrew. "'As It Was in the Beginning': Organ and Choir Pitch in Early Anglican Church Music." *Early Music* 31 (2003): 507–25.

Kenyon, Nicholas, ed. *Authenticity and Early Music: A Symposium.* London: Oxford University Press, 1988.

Kite-Powell, Jeffrey T., ed. *A Performer's Guide to Renaissance Music.* New York: Schirmer, 1994.

Kivy, Peter. *Authenticities: Philosophical Reflections on Musical Performance.* Ithaca, N.Y.: Cornell University Press, 1995.

Knighton, Tess, and David Fallows, eds. *Companion to Medieval and Renaissance Music.* New York: Schirmer, 1992.

Kreitner, Kenneth. "Bad News or Not? Thoughts on Renaissance Performance Practice." *Early Music* 26 (1998): 323–25.

———. "Very Low Ranges in the Sacred Music of Ockeghem and Tinctoris." *Early Music* 14 (1986): 467–79.

Kurtzman, Jeffery. *The Monteverdi Vespers of 1610: Music, Context, and Performance.* Oxford and New York: Oxford University Press, 1999.

Letters of Mozart and His Family. Translated by Emily Anderson. New York: W. W. Norton, 1989.

Lionnet, Jean. "Performance Practice in the Papal Chapel during the 17th Century." *Early Music* 15 (1987): 3–15.

Lowinsky, Edward. "Music of the Renaissance as Viewed by Renaissance Musicans." In *The Renaissance Image of Man and the World,* edited by Bernard O'Kelly. Columbus: Ohio State University Press, 1966.

MacClintock, Carol. *Readings in the History of Music in Performance.* Bloomington: Indiana University Press, 1979.

McGee, Timothy J. *Medieval and Renaissance Music: A Performer's Guide.* Toronto: University of Toronto Press, 1985.

———. *Singing Early Music.* Bloomington: Indiana University Press, 1996.

Mersenne, Marin. *Harmonie Universelle: The Books on Instruments.* Translated by Roger E. Chapman. The Hague: Martinus Nijhoff, 1957.

Mertin, Josef. *Early Music: Approaches to Performance Practice.* Translated by Siegmund Levarie. Irig, 1978; reprint, New York: Da Capo Press, 1986.

Miller, Richard. *English, French, German and Italian Techniques of Singing.* Metuchen, N.J.: Scarecrow Press, 1977.

Moore, James H. "The *Vespro delle Cinque Laudate* and the Role of *Salmi Spezzati* at St. Mark's." *Journal of the American Musicological Society* 34 (1981): 249–78.

Morehen, John, ed. *English Choral Practice 1400–1650.* Cambridge: Cambridge University Press, 1995.

Nagler, A. M. *Theatre Festivals of the Medici, 1534–1637.* Translated by George Hickenlooper. New Haven, Conn.: Yale University Press, 1964.

North, Roger. *Notes of Me: The Autobiography of Roger North,* edited by Peter Millard. Toronto: University of Toronto Press, 2000.

Parrott, Andrew. *The Essential Bach Choir.* New York: Boydell Press, 2000.

———. "Grett and Solompne Singing: Instruments in English Church Music before the Civil War." *Early Music* 6 (1978): 182–87.

———. "Transposition in Monteverdi's Vespers of 1610: An 'Aberration' Defended." *Early Music* 12 (1984): 490–516.

Phillips, Peter. "The Golden Age Regained." *Early Music* 8 (1980): 3–16, 180–98.

Postman, Neil. *Amusing Ourselves to Death.* New York: Penguin, 1985.

Potter, John, ed. *The Cambridge Companion to Singing.* Cambridge: Cambridge University Press, 2000.

———. *Vocal Authority: Singing Style and Ideology.* Cambridge: Cambridge University Press, 1988.

Prosdocimo de' Beldomandi. *Contrapunctus.* Translated by Jan Herlinger. Lincoln: University of Nebraska Press, 1984.

Ravens, Simon. "A Sweet Shrill Voice: The Countertenor and Vocal Scoring in Tudor England." *Early Music* 26 (1998): 122–34.

Rosselli, John. "The Castrati as a Professional Group and a Social Phenomenon, 1550–1850." *Acta Musicologica* 60 (1988): 143–79.

Routley, Nicholas. "A Practical Guide to *musica ficta*." *Early Music* 13 (1985): 59–71.

Sachs, Curt. *Rhythm and Tempo*. New York: W. W. Norton, 1953.

Sandborg, Jeffrey. *English Ways*. Chapel Hill, N.C.: Hinshaw Music, 2001.

Sanford, Sally. "A Comparison of French and Italian Singing in the Seventeenth Century." *Journal of Seventeenth-Century Music* 1 (1995), available at sscm-jscm.press.uiuc.edu/jscm/v1no1.html.

———. "Seventeenth- and Eighteenth-Century Vocal Style and Technique." DMA diss., Stanford University, 1979.

"Scholarship & Performance: Peter Phillips Interviews Bruno Turner." *Early Music* 6 (1978): 199–203.

Segerman, Ephraim. "A Re-examination of the Evidence on Absolute Tempo before 1700." *Early Music* 24 (1996): 227–48.

Sherman, Bernard. *Inside Early Music: Conversations with Performers*. New York: Oxford University Press, 1997.

Sherr, Richard. "Performance Practice in the Papal Chapel during the 16th Century." *Early Music* 15 (1987): 453–62.

Slim, H. Colin. "Francesco da Milano (1497–1543/44): A Biographical and Bibliographical Study, I." *Musica Disciplina* 18 (1964): 63–84.

Smithers, Don L. *The Music and History of the Baroque Trumpet before 1721*. Carbondale: Southern Illinois University Press, 1988.

Somville, Marilyn Elizabeth Feller. "Vowels and Consonants as Factors in Early Singing Style and Technique." Ph.D. diss., Stanford University, 1967.

Sternfeld, F. W. "Aspects of Italian Intermedi and Early Opera." In *Convivium musicorum: Festschrift Wolfgang Boetticher zum sechzigsten Geburtstag am 19 August 1974*. Berlin: Verlag Merseburger, 1974.

Strunk, Oliver, ed. *Source Readings in Music History*. New York: W. W. Norton, 1950.

Taruskin, Richard. *Text and Act: Essays on Music and Performance*. New York: Oxford University Press, 1995.

Tatnall, Roland. "Falsetto Practice: A Brief Survey." *The Consort* 22 (1965): 311–35.

Tinctoris, Johannes. *Dictionary of Musical Terms*. Translated by Carl Parrish. New York: Free Press of Glencoe (1963).

Treitler, Leo, ed. *Strunk's Source Readings in Music History*. New York: W. W. Norton, 1998.

Ulrich, Bernhard. *Concerning the Principles of Voice Training during the A Cappella Period and until the Beginning of Opera (1474–1640)*. Translated by John W. Seale. Minneapolis, Minn.: Pro Musica Press, 1973.

Vicentino, Nicola. *Ancient Music Adapted to Modern Practice*. Translated by Maria Rika Maniates. New Haven, Conn.: Yale University Press, 1996.

von Ramm, Andrea. "Singing Early Music." *Early Music* 4 (1976): 12–15.

Wegman, Rob. "Sense and Sensibility in Late-Medieval Music." *Early Music* 23 (1995): 299–312.

Weiner, Howard. "The Soprano Trombone Hoax." *Historic Brass Society Journal* 13 (2001): 138–60.

Wulstan, David. *Tudor Music.* London: Dent, 1985.

———. "Vocal Colour in English Sixteenth-Century Polyphony." *Journal of the Plainsong & Mediaeval Music Society* 2 (1979): 19–60.

Zarlino, Gioseffo. *On the Modes: Part Four of Le Istitutioni Harmoniche, 1558.* Translated by Vered Cohen. New Haven, Conn.: Yale University Press, 1983.

Index

About the Author

Steven E. Plank is director of the Collegium Musicum Oberliniense and professor of musicology at Oberlin College (Ohio). He is the author of *The Way to Heavens Doore: An Introduction to Liturgical Process and Musical Style* (1994), and has contributed articles to *Music & Letters, Early Music,* and *The Musical Times.* He has also been an Anglican church musician for thirty years.